Dyslexia

Best wishes

Lance

Live it to know it!

By Lance Rose
lancerose@hotmail.co.uk

Thanks to

My Partner Corinne without whom this book would only be a dream.

I'd also like to thank Helen Jones and Hazel Spencer for all of their help.

INTRODUCTION

People around me thought they knew me! They could see a man who was fazed by nothing. A man standing 6 feet tall, weighing 15 and a half stone, with arms of iron, bearded and feral, with a gypsy charm and striking blue eyes to match.
A man who feared nothing, that same man with unquestionable confidence.
A man with out a care in the world, who had achieved big goals in his life.
A man with numerous crafts in his hands.
He has friends in every town and village, friends that ranged from farm labourers, through to mechanics, vets, millionaire business men to aero engineers. They had all seen me building my house from the ground up, dressing the stone, and placing every one on top of the last.

They had watched as I built a successful business for myself. They had heard the quick wit. But they really didn't know me at all, yes I guess I was all of those things on the surface, but I had got really good at covering up my handicap, the handicap that had on the one hand held me back yet on the other pushed me hard to achieve my goals.

THE HANDICAP, THE SECRET IS "DYSLEXIA"!

I have always believed that we are all put on this planet for a reason, I cant tell you why I should think this way but it just seems the way things are to me, but for a hell of along time I couldn't figure out what my reason was!
Then I taught myself how to read and write after years in the darkness and

frustration of dyslexia!
I found answers to questions that had held me back for years,
had I found my reason?
May be just may be this could be the reason!

I might not be able to change the worlds misunderstanding of dyslexia but if I can shine a little light on how it is for the sufferers then the problems might be a little easer remedied.

So I have to tell the teachers there is a way!

I have to show them all how it feels for that bright kid who just doesn't read or write so well!

I have to show them ALL there is a way!

I have to show them that the kid with dyslexia could be better understood!

I have got to try and some how banish the stigma of dyslexia!

I have got to help that kid that just doesn't understand!

I have got to tell the mother of that dyslexic kid there is hope!

I have got to somehow stop that unintentional abuse!

FOR THAT KID, WHO WAS ME, I WRITE THIS BOOK!

Chapter 1

The story so far,

I live in a stone barn in a beautiful Derbyshire village, which I converted from a dark dank and derelict wreck, along with my partner corinne and my seventeen year old son Sid, people told us we were mad to take on such a task, but after three years of hard labour, transforming a building that was not fit to house livestock, apart from the resident rodents;
no water, electricity, not even a roof to speak of to the end result that is a family home to be proud of, with its farm house kitchen and cosy log fires and an extra deep bath to soak the aching muscles at the end of the day, they change there tune!

The barn is surrounded by twelve acres of unspoilt pasture land that is ever changing through the seasons, spring brings the vibrant colours, blue bells, yellow of daffodils, the clean white of the snowdrops, and as if to tell us its spring once more the birds sing there songs in the pink red and white blossom of the hawthorn, black thorn, crab apple that all in turn brings the unmistakable sent of the season,

Lambs in the fields and the lengthening days putting an end to the long dark nights of winter and with it those cosy evenings spent by that roaring log fire for one more year.

And as spring turns to summer the sent changes to the smell of the tree pollen and of cause the unmistakable smell of freshly cut grass. Pheasants barking, wood pigeons cooing, and the welcome return that is to me at least the very essence of summer the swallow sitting chatting about its long journey on the phone wires that I'm sure they think have been put there purely for there benefit, and there they sit, it seems, all summer chatting about the price of lamb, how big the foal has grown and how its been a good year for the hay, but with the changing colour of the leaves on the trees and the misty mornings that signifies the end of summer they are gone as quickly as they came and we are in to autumn before we know it, time once more to baton down the hatches against the winter winds and snow and like squirrels feverishly filling there winter stores we harvest the fruits of our labour to see us though the winter months, well maybe Sainsburys is more like it for us but we gather winter fodder for the horses, hay straw carrots and corn.

We built American style stables, a big building with internal boxes for our shire horses down one side and carriage store and tack room on the other;
life for me has never been better, Corinne and myself trained the shires to work on our land and we pull logs out of other peoples woods when requested, along with

weddings and carriage rides, I guess to describe it as a job would be the truth but to us its more like a passion, and we share our passion with others people who are not as fortunate to have our life style, and they pay us to do so,
although it can be very hard work, in my view it don't get much better than this,
we recently spent 48 sleepless hours foaling a mare that had with its previously owner lost its last two foals,
we took our lives in our own hands when we were faced with a shire mare that stands 18 hands high, "you don't get many horses much bigger than that" we had got to hand milk, especially as we had been warned that she could be hateful when she had a foal at foot! Which is only natural, she only wants to protect her baby from nasty predators and she doesn't know that we are only trying to help, never the less we had been warned: And although she hadn't as yet got the foal at foot we knew she could be what is

only natural, "hateful"! but its all worth the effort to see "Cassie" lying in the field along side her mum taking in the warmth of the afternoon sun,
lying there without a care in the world.

The book that you are about to read was written solely by yours truly, and when I say written by me I mean by me, no ghost writers no fancy classes, just me and my laptop with no formal training, in fact no training formal or other wise!
I guess that sounds like some big headed boast!
and I suppose it is!
but for some thirty-six years of my life I was unable to read or write the most simple of words, and sentences were completely out of the question, so if I sound a little big headed then I'm sorry but I must admit that I am intensely proud of what I have achieved in the last few years, I'm even proud of the naff punctuation and the spelling mistakes

that I have chosen to leave in, I didn't want some one coming in and changing my text and not only that I think rightly or wrongly it makes my book more personal.

when I started writing I wanted to show you just how hard life can be for me and other dyslexics, so I have tried to give you the truth as personal as that may be all the way through my text.
For many years I had hung my head in shame, in the shame that is dyslexia!
The stigma of not reading or writing and the way that is perceived was always present in my life.

For years I had ducked dived blagged and lied my way through sticky situations that could of expose me to ridicule because of my dyslexia, so one or two spelling mistakes although not very professional are nothing in comparison from where I started.

As I sit here I have just turned 49 years old, and I can tell you there have been times when I thought I wouldn't make it, life hasn't always been easy!

The Friends that surrounded me now had no idea of what to me was a shameful past, I was careful not to let them know of my childhood or my youth. How I had been put into a no hope class at school, how the people who surrounded me then thought of me as a fool, a misfit and stupid, how hard life had been then, a kid lost and forgotten cocooned in his shell trying to break free but no one would listen, no one could understand or help me, I was as scared now as I had been then, if they knew of my dyslexia they would think of it as just another word for stupid! I had managed to build respect from my friends but I was always worried that one day they would find me out and that respect and credibility would be lost for ever.

How would it be accepted by them if they knew of my school days, how I was put in a class of kids that really needed help, or at home how I was even less understood so I was the fool that did all the menial tasks.

I could write my name but my address was an uphill struggle!
This had got to change and change fast, so I would sit alone night after night trying to sort my dyslexia out, and after months and years trying I thought I had cracked it, so I tried my theory out on one of my sons friends that I knew was dyslexic, and it did work!

As I sit in front of my laptop I feel privileged that I have a story to share with you, the story that is my life struggle and mastery of dyslexia.

Chapter 2

LIVE IT TO KNOW IT.

So I'm dyslexic, and can I start by saying its not terminal you know!!
i know that might sound like a strange thing to say but you would think it is judging by peoples reaction to it:
yes it's a desperate situation and it can be one hell of an obstacle in life, but its not going to kill you or anyone around you.
I have suffered from dyslexia all my life but looking back I wouldn't of had it any other way!!
The fact is however I'm dyslexic no getting away from it "DYSLEXIC"
So with that fact established,
I'm going to start from the end of this book!
Well what did you expect??
As a dyslexic I have the right!
After all everything is back to front for a dyslexic isn't it?
If only things were that simple but it gives me the right anyway.

Joking apart there is a dam good reason why I should start from the end of this book, well towards the end anyway;
I hope that you will of learned how to make reading and writing easier by the time you get to the end of my text yourself but for now just try what I say.

So for those of you who are dyslexic and trying to read this book my first word of advice is to just read the words!
Sound simple and daft???
Well it will do!
Let me give you a brief explanation, and I will explain more later but for now bare with me.
we as dyslexics see in pictures, so a word that has a picture is easier for us to recognise than a word with no picture.
and just to confuse us as you know not all words have pictures, in fact there are a lot more words that don't have pictures than do.
Quick examples 'ball', has a picture, 'at',

has no picture, and 'to', 'two', or 'too', are just confusing.

Its as if we need to see the picture before the letters on the page make any sense at all,

So every time you read a word you ask your brain to give you a picture for that word, which is fine if you read the word ball, your brain comes back with the picture, it's a beach ball its blue and white, or it's a football and its black and white, you see what I'm getting at, you have a clear picture of the ball.

But believe me when I say if you ask your brain subconsciously for pictures for words like "at as is if of" you could look for days and your brain will never come back with a picture for those words, but you are relentless with your insistence for a picture, and by the time your brain has given up looking you have lost your flow of what you were reading and nothing will make sense, or at least it will be heavy going.

If I was sat with you right now the question that I would ask is,
When you read or even attempt to read do you start fine then run out of fuel the farther you get in to the sentence?
And do you have to read the sentence ten times before it makes sense? If so chances are you are wasting time and energy looking for pictures, so as I say stop wasting time and just read the word, it will make life a whole lot easier, consciously tell yourself not to look for pictures before you attempt to read, and give yourself reminders from time to time as you go.

At this point you don't need to know why or how it works, just give it a go and I know you will be surprised at the difference.

Looking for pictures takes time and effort that could be better spent just reading and understanding the word.

Hopefully if you try to do as I say your reading will become easier and you wont have to read the whole book ten times to understand it.

Chapter 3

So now for the start!

But where do I start!

Well I'm no big wig boffin or shrink. Just a man who has lived the nightmare of dyslexia and I've come out the other side,

I SPENT YEARS LOOKING FOR ANSWERS TO THE PUZZLE THAT HAD PLAGUED ME FOR MOST OF MY LIFE.

No one could help me with my hardest life struggle!
No one could understand!
Specialists, experts, psychologists, teachers,
I saw them all but no one could help!
So I had to help myself,
I had no other option!

The saying is you have to live it to know it!

A dyslexic couldn't help me as they didn't understand WHY they couldn't read write or understand the written word themselves let alone help me!
And non dyslexics couldn't help as I was soon to find out they too didn't understand either;
how could they after all they are not dyslexic, they didn't see what I was seeing, if that makes sense?
If not hopefully it will later!

To my knowledge the problem is still vastly misunderstood, ok dyslexia is more readily acknowledged now days but that's not to say its better understood, I hear storeys of so called specialists still using tools that I know at best don't help and at worst make things more difficult.
I've never heard of a specialist who is truly dyslexic himself,
to my mind that's like asking a gardener to teach you how to fly an aeroplane, quit obviously the wrong man

to show you how, just as it would be to ask a non dyslexic to teach a dyslexic, I know they all profess to have studied dyslexia and have the answers, but I know as living proof they don't!!!
I had to become my own expert, specialist, and therapist, I had to do it for myself.

what constituts an expert anyway?

How can anyone be considered an expert in anything that they have never experienced?

How could we respect a driving instructor who doesn't have a driving licence? Or a swimming instructor who cant swim? I hope at least the non driver wouldn't even consider becoming a driving instructor, or a non swimmer becoming a swimming instructor, I know I'm over simplifying things but you can see what im getting at!

we hope that nothing as ridicules as that

would happen or shouldn't at least, but nothing would surprise me in this day and age, but that is just what we have in my view when we set non dyslexics to teach dyslexics.
It really is the blind leading the blind.
It would be a ridicules thing to suggest that a true dyslexic go in to teaching, especially teaching English!

I mean someone who was in my position not able to write or spell my address as a true dyslexic!

I don't have to explain that the dyslexic in that position wouldn't have the qualifications to become a teacher do I.

so as a consequence we have the inexperienced trying to teach that innocent kid who up until recently didn't know they had this massive problem.
I'm not suggesting that we employ

dyslexics as English teachers, far from it, but I do think that the so called experts accept that while they might be a big help , they will never be the expert they had thought, and they could do a lot worse than listen to the dyslexic, to those who qualify as experts by experience.

I guess I have to put my views on teachers as I have experienced them both then "in my day" and as I see things today, in this book. So as I say in my view as a dyslexic who has been there and lived the nightmare. Teachers back then in my day I can excuse for there ignorance. But now today, I know they could learn such a lot if only they would listen to those of us who qualify by experience.
But that's an up hill struggle, every teacher I have ever tried to talk to has had an arrogance that they are right. I can see that it's got to be hard for a teacher of many years experience to accept they could of done things better or that they

might have been wrong all this time.

The answers I get when I tell them how it was for me and how I had to teach myself, are its so much different now days, things have changed so much in the past thirty years, and yes it probably has but different doesn't necessarily mean better! If it was that much better why is it that we still have kids leaving school today not being able to read and write? and how is it that I can help these kids if all that can be done is being done?
Further more if that is the case and everything is being done then why have you bought this book?

Clearly its not and in my experience the experts don't like a redneck like me telling them that there might be a better way!
And I can understand that, they have spent years studying to gain there qualifications then along I come without

a single official qualification and tell them there might be a better way, but after all I have been inadvertently studying dyslexia all my life!

I know at one time "my time" teachers that had heard of dyslexia just thought it was another word for stupid, and I dare say there are still a few who think the same way today,
but I'd lived for years with that dark shadow of dyslexia or should I say "stupidity" hanging over me, with shame of not being able to read or write, and with an overwhelming feeling that I had let everyone around me down, and as strange as it may seem I still have that feeling running through my veins today;
I felt that I had caused everyone around me heart aches, problems, and pain, not true I know and I know it's not my fault, its just the way things are but the feeling lingers on.

As I sit here and read that last statement as you do! I felt it needs better describing and the only comparison I can think of is when you are accused of something that you didn't do but you cant prove you didn't! try this one, the local garage proprietor has over the years become a friend of yours and you take your car In for it annual service and the service is a set price witch you pay as you drop the car off, but when you go to pick up your car later your friend the proprietor hands you a bill!

But you know you paid earlier it was £132 and you paid in cash you even remember taking the cash out of your wallet and you even remember witch pocket he put it in but you have no proof! How do you defend yourself and how can you prove you have paid? You have no cheque stub or receipt so you cant! Your friend now thinks you are trying to rip him off and you think the same of him, but you know you paid but then you start to question yourself, did I pay? Is it me who is at fault or him? And you have to take the car to him next time just to show you have no shame or feeling of guilt but that's just a front you do feel guilty even through you know your not and everything becomes strained;

You get the picture, you question yourself when you know the truth, but every time you see your friend you know he thinks you are a bad payer, end result shame and a feeling of guilt when you know you are in the right, well that's similar to the guilt I still feel today, but as I say only similar, in reality its worse than that !!

that same feeling of guilt runs over into a feeling of not belonging;

I never really fitted in anywhere, to use the word outcast may be a bit strong but it is the best word to describe how I felt. But an outcast is what I was, no one around me was dyslexic and no one could understand what was wrong with me.

Chapter 4

They say NEVER JUDGE OR CRITICISE A MAN UNTIL YOU HAVE WALKED A MILE IN HIS SHOES!

I've walked the mile in the dyslexics shoes and I've felt the crippling pain, (that pain of letting the people around you down, the people you really love) I've heard the heart wrenching comments (dyslexic hey? More like plane stupid, said by people who should of known better) and I've seen peoples reactions to the fool that cant read or write too many bloody times, (parents dragging there kids away like I had some infectious disease) and I've been let down by the best experts and specialists you could find, so in my opinion that alone gives me all the qualifications I need to write this book.

As adults we can understand the meaning in the above statement but as a kid it doesn't make sense, just as it

doesn't when you tell a kid that is as sharp as a razor they have a problem.
If he is not being told directly that he's stupid he will be feeling it by the way he is now being treated.
For a kid who didn't know he/she had a problem it can be very painful and confusing.

He can run almost as fast as his big brother he can ride his bike, brush his teeth, put his toys away tidy his room, and always remembers his manners, but he still got the vibes that not all is well from his teachers, mum and dad, and as far as he can see is its all his fault, but what had he done wrong? He's not smashed a window or hit his little sister so what had he done?
And to make matters worse he has to give up his precious play time to spend time with the expert like some kind of punishment, so not only had it taken away his free time but it has shown all

his mates that he has a problem to, and the pressure just keeps getting greater and greater.

Let me give you an example, and this is a story that i hear time and time again.

I was talking recently to a mother (I'll call her Sharon) of a dyslexic girl (and I'll call her Abby) about the help she was giving her daughter.
I've changed the names to save embarrassment!
Sharon was feeling disappointed that the help she was giving Abby was just not working, and asked me what I thought she was doing wrong.
After chatting for a while it soon became obvious to me that in Sharon's eagerness to help she was putting so much psychological pressure on Abby with her teaching technique, but I could also see that on the face of it what Sharon was doing sounds really good and helpful.

She told me that every night after school she would take the time to sit with Abby at the kitchen table with a list of words that Abby had to read to her mother.

The list would comprise of thirty words at the most, but she said that it just wasn't working and if anything Abby was getting worse, she told me that the problem that Abby had must be worse than she had first thought, and that she thought Abby had a behaviour problem to, her tantrums were getting worse, she thought Abby was a little ungrateful so and so, and she was thinking of giving up on the whole idea of being able to help. She asked me what more could she do as she was getting desperate and she really needed to help.

As I say sounds like the mother was trying her best, and I was thinking well what more could she do? I'm sure you will agree what more could she do?

She's taking valuable time out of her busy day to give as much support to Abby as she could, she really was trying her very best to help.

But as is always the case in these things there are two sides to these stories, so I asked how many of the words Abby would get correct?

And the initial reply was, well it started out that maybe she would get half of them right but its getting worse the more we do, and the words are no more difficult than at the start! Four months of work and she is getting no better.

All the time she was telling me this I could see she was welling up with the emotion of it all, and I remembered my own experience of this, my mother would sit with me to, in pretty much the same circumstances at the kitchen table, and I remembered the pressure I felt in that situation, if I got a word right I would be praised but if I got it wrong I would get "no that's wrong try again but this time try" or i dont understand you, you read that one last night and got it right! after a while all I could focus on was the praise or the punishment and not on the word and as a consequence I got more and more wrong until one day my mum gave up, and i felt it was all my fault. I guess in her eyes it was she just couldn't see the pressure I was under, it is beyond most peoples comprehension that the written word could be so difficult to understand and she was no exception. as i say she just didnt understand, she had tried her heart out but had been met with a wall of frustration.

What I didn't know at the time was that I couldn't even recognise the letters never mind the words, but you will hear more about that later.
So back to Sharon and Abby,
I could see that my situation as it was to turn out was the reverse of Abby's but the

end result was the same PRESSURE!
May be Sharon just didn't understand, the same as my mum hadn't!
I asked what Sharon did when Abby got a word right? And the answer was what I expected, she would hug and kiss her, but then I asked what she would do if she got them wrong? And the answer was what I expected to,
she didn't do anything apart from telling her she had got it wrong, and moved straight on to the next word, and I guess the part that was omitted from Sharon's answer and something that she couldn't express to me in words and that is the look of disappointment and despair on her face, that look that I'm sure by now Abby knew only to well.
So in effect what she was doing was restricting her affection every time the wrong answer was given and punishing her, when all the girl wanted to do was get the word right, please her mum and win hugs and a kiss.

I could see that it would be really difficult for Sharon to hide her disappointment when the wrong answer was given but maybe she could curb her elation when the right answer was given! I also pointed out surely praise was disserved for just trying!

I pointed out that she might as well slap Abby in the face every time she got a word wrong if she wasn't going to praise her for at least trying!
After all Abby was trying to get all the words right and she was putting just as much effort in to every one, but what she was getting if she got one wrong was in effect a slap in the face, I felt I had to point this out to Sharon and immediately she could see the pressure she was piling on the girl was immense and it would make the most simple of words that much more difficult.

Can you imagine how that girl would be

feeling at that split second of judgement, the look of expectation in her eyes as she awaited her fate? If it was right she got hugs and kisses and what's more she knew her mum was proud of her, but if it was wrong nothing not even well done for trying, plain and simple NOTHING! Gut wrenching heart breaking disappointing NOTHING!

It was really difficult for me to tell a loving and caring mother who was doing her best that she was making the whole thing more difficult. But I had been asked my opinion and I felt that I had to give it for Abby's sake.
I could see the situation in its self was stressful enough, it was already like a punishment, Abby had an older sister that didn't suffer from dyslexia and she wasn't dragged away from the T.V. or her pony to sit and do yet more schooling after school, Sharon told me that the lessons took priority over everything else,

the lesson had to be completed before Abby was aloud to play, again I could see Sharon wanted to help and I could see it was important for her to help her daughter she loved and cared so much for, but on the other hand I could see it from Abby's side,

Abby was ten years old and all she wanted to do was play but her play time was being radically reduced by these well meaning sessions with her mother at the kitchen table, I can hear Abby screaming out **WHY ME?**

WHY DON'T YOU GET OFF MY CASE AND LEAVE ME ALONE?

IV DONE NOTHING WRONG BUT IM GETTING PUNISHED!

WHY ME AND NOT MY SISTER??? ITS NOT FAIR!

And its not fair but the most painful

side to it for me was no one was listening to her screams.

She wanted and now she needed someone to help her but as far as she could see all she was getting was punishment.

I pointed this out to Sharon and told her to relax the whole situation, after all how would she like to be told to go and do half an hour ironing before she could watch her favourite T.V. program??

I told her of my experience sat with my mum at the kitchen table, I gave her some tips on what Abby might be struggling with and I told her not to be so extreme with her verdict, I pointed out that even with the words Abby was getting wrong the effort was just as great so the praise should be the same for each word, so cut her some slack and that way the pressure would be radically reduced and the girl could get on with the job in hand, reading.

I told her to change the time! maybe she could hold the sessions when

there was nothing on the T.V. or when it was raining outside, and it would be better to have one good relaxed session than ten stressful ones.
I guess as I look at the situation as it was I must fall short of calling it abuse, intentional abuse anyway, but maybe unintentional abuse and only then because it was done in ignorance and innocence.

As it is in many of these cases Abby was a very bright kid, polite and courteous with a smile that could melt your heart,
I was pleased that I had been asked my opinion and with it was able to help a ten year old girl, and rescue her from that stressful situation, and yes I think RESCUE is the right word to use!
but you know through all of this there is one underlying thing that all the parants are guilty of and that is love of there kids, and an unshakable will to help, if they didnt care they would do

nothing but that's not always understood by there children.

Chapter 5

Sometimes it will take something really big, an event in our lives that we just weren't prepared for to make us look at the way our lives have developed.

Something that will make us say to ourselves enough is enough.

Nothing ever stays the same for long, all of us will go through life changing situations in the course of our lives we will all at some stage be faced with and have to cope with unforeseen circumstances and maybe more than once.
we will at some point find ourselves in a place where we feel all hope is lost, or maybe the change could be an exciting new start, a new beginning, but I guess that depends on your stand point in life, and of course the situation itself;

Things that make us stop and look at the way our lives have evolved.

The things that make us remember the dreams, and aspirations we had when we were younger.

some of the biggest changes and challenges, the biggest things to stop us and make us take stock of where our lives are going, for anyone must be the loss of a loved one.
and there's divorce,
changing your job,
emigrating,
having kids,
retirement,
illness,
exams at school or collage,
all to some degree life changing, situations we all may face at some point in our lives, and we can only sympathise with that person who has just lost a parent, or is going through a divorce, we can see that there world has just been turned upside down.

Or the euphoria of a fantastic new promotion,
the shear excitement of moving abroad and starting a new life.

but until we have lived the said situation that's all we can do, sympathise or imagine the feeling of elation at that promotion, the delight of becoming a parent for the first time, or maybe that's the way we are programmed to look at life, what if the person is being forced to move abroad through no choice of there own and is just putting on a brave face!
Or maybe that promotion will put a lot more pressure and stress on them when really all they want to do is buy a little cottage in the country and write poetry, but it's the right thing to do for the sake of there family,
And what if you just don't feel ready to become a parent,
What I'm getting at is that we have to

live a situation before we can have any clue as to how it truly feels, and we can never really be sure how we are going to react when faced with life changing situations.

we all know that at some stage in life we will lose someone close to us but we try not to think of it, its to painful to contemplate, but out of that situation we are faced with and cope with things we thought were beyond our capabilities, but now that the mantle is thrust into our hand we find the strength and courage from somewhere to cope, maybe because we have no other choice but to cope.
Or it could be that for some reason we are made redundant and at the time it's the end of the world to you, but it could be that it was just the thing needed to push you into setting up that business you had always dreamed of, but just never got the opportunity while you were

employed, your job had paid the mortgage, the bills, fed the kids, paid the HP on the car, and so on, but now you have no choice, it might be the only realistic option you have or the only chance you ever get and you've been pushed in to it, you might never of done it if not for being made redundant, and it could be after setting up your business you wished you had done it years ago, what I'm saying is we just don't know how we will react!

And again you might not have done as well and got the grades in you're A levels that you were expecting and didn't get in to the university you had set your heart on, or maybe you got the grades then university but just didn't get offered the right job, then end up stacking shelves in the local supermarket, or maybe you did get the grades but ended up doing something completely unrelated to you're qualifications, that you really enjoy, or that your divorce was a devastating shock at the time but after time you can look back and see it was the best thing for all concerned, it might be that now you find yourself in a situation that is better suited to you after all, but in all of these situations its rare that we see it at the time.

We just don't know where the roller coaster of life is going to take us next, and we all react differently to any given situation,

So as I say you have to live it to know it, we have to feel the heat before we know how hot it really is.

I had just turned thirty when my dad suddenly died, and I guess as I look back I can now see that he had been the only member of my family who I could relate to, and again in reflection I can see that I handle situations in very similar ways. We had the same sense of humour, I'm told I have the same outlook on life, he was the only person I have ever admired and not just because he was my dad, I admired the man, his razor sharp mind, his lightening wit, his thirst for knowledge but most of all was his unconventional approach to life.

I remember working along side him when I was in my early teens, he had been asked to take a tree down that was becoming dangerous leaning towards a house, the seen was my brother was on the chainsaw I was lookout and norm as I called him was in the land rover keeping tension on a rope that we had attached to the tree as a means of safety. A crowd had gathered to watch, as the chain saw sliced through the tree norm would keep trying the tension on the rope just to make sure the tree was heading the right way, just at a crucial moment one of my former teachers walked up to the window of the land rover and said to norm "trees are stronger than you think" to witch he replied how strong do you think I think trees are? The guy stood there in a daze for a while trying to work out what he had just been told. I think he got it in the end but that was it the time my dad became my idol! Maybe it was that he had just made that teacher who had made me look a fool look foolish himself or maybe just his fast thinking or even both, but never the less he was the one person I looked up to. It was him that had shown me that there were no wrong moves in life but just learning curves and that some were steeper than others. No wrong moves just as long as we learn from them. My only regret is that I didn't learn more about the way his mind worked and why while he was still around, but he had taught me that bad news was not necessarily bad, it could turn out after all to be good news but it could be that you just didn't see it at the time.

His death had been a massive shock to me and I missed him desperately.

If you were to of asked me if I could have been one of his pallbearers while he was still around I would of said without question NO, I thought that that would be a situation I just couldn't cope with, but at the end that's exactly what I did, I did it with pride and I'm pleased I did.
But my friend had gone and I would never see his face again, hear his laughter, or have a conversation with him,
As I say he was the only one in my family who I could relate, but I only realised that when he had gone, and now I look back and I can see just how alike we really are, but I don't think he could understand me, he hadn't taught me any thing directly, I would watch from a far as he would teach my older brother, and at the time I didn't really appreciate just how much I was taking in, but he

had while he was around unwittingly given me the strength to cope with life's trials.

Then six years later I was faced with divorce and divorce is rarely a nice experience my own was no exception,
with all the acrimony, lies and rumours about who had done what and why, and of course the obligatory solicitors, together with the realisation that a friend of mine turned out to be more than just a friend to my wife.
I had found myself in a desperate situation, I was again alone but I was 36 years old, and I had still not faced my handicap but now I had solicitors letters to read, bills to pay, cheques to write, forms to fill out, all the things that at this point in my life were impossible, the things that I would rely on my wife to do for me but by now she was long gone.

I had just completed building a magnificent four bed roomed house, that I had been working on for the past eighteen months, putting in fourteen hours a day, seven days a week, when I realised just what was going on, I guess I had been too busy to see just what was happening between them, but the up shot of it all was my wife had gone with her toy boy who was fifteen years younger than me and ten years younger than her! And that doesn't do your man hood much good I can tell you, but it was never going to last and it didn't, but by that time the marriage was over.

but the hardest part for me to bare, together with the anger that I had been made to look a real fool, was that she had taken my six year old son Sid with her and I missed him desperately, he had been with me in his overalls and with his own little spade insisting on helping, and yes sometimes he would get under my feet, but now he had gone through no choice of his own and I would only get to see him twice a week for two or if I was really lucky three hours, for the rest of the time I didn't know where he was, how he was. I didn't even know if he was well, or if he was happy or sad, and every time he had visited it was never long enough, I had become a weekend dad like lots more, and every time I close the door behind him when he had gone I would dissolve in to floods of tear's, enough to destroy a man,

I never really got use to it, but after time hard as it was I got to accept it, I'd tried to gain better access but was told by my solicitor that I had very little chance as the court almost always awarded the mother the custody and with it the decisions, especially in situations where mothers don't work so without a long and hard court battle I had to accept what I got.

I was already racked with guilt that the

marriage had failed and we were putting Sid through pain and heart ache that he just didn't deserve, he didn't understand why his mum and dad no longer lived together so I wasn't about to put him through a tug of war custody battle,
But when he was thirteen and old enough to make his own decisions he came to live with me, and is again my right hand man, my best friend, so out of this horrible situation some good at last had come my way, so again as I say that roller coaster had a hell of a switch back and its not always bad.

They say an English mans home is his castle and I had had this vision of how mine would look for years, and it had taken me over ten years, searching far and wide, firstly to find a place where I could see my home " the vision" and one that I could afford, then when I had eventually found the place the next stage and the hardest was gaining planning consent for my vision to be able to become a reality, the place I had found was fifteen Acres of land on the hillside that is the Derwent valley, over looking the river Derwent gently making its way south, and shining cliff woods with its ever changing canopy of colours, it was a magnificent view and from the first moment I set foot on the place it felt right and I knew I had found the place I wanted to be, but the local councils planning department had got a completely different idea and at every opportunity put whatever obstacle they could think of in my way. But they hadn't accounted on my stubborn persistence, and with every obstacle I somehow found an answer, and eventually I gained the consent I had been working towards, then I had sweat blood and tears building my house, to make my vision a reality and it had already cost me a high price as regards my health, I had worked so hard and long on my beautiful home that I would never feel quite the same again, but now I was being forced to sell it and my dreams were all in tatters.

It all contributed to a very stressful and unpleasant time,
But as I look back and hear other people's experiences my divorce was as normal as they get, and I can now see the funny side of some of the things that were said and done, I might be a lot of things but I had to laugh when Jane's solicitors sent me a letter accusing me of being gay, I had been out for the night(to a truck racing presentation that I had been involved with) and realised I couldn't get home in time to be there to receive Sid, so I had rang and asked a good friend of mine Phil if he would go and sit at my house in time for Sid's arrival, I told him where I had hidden the spare key and for him to make himself at

home and that I wouldn't be long, but the letter said that if I couldn't be home to receive my own son then could I not have my boyfriend do the job for me! I'd been accused of a lot of things through the divorce but never gay, I guess it was designed to make me mad but all I could do was laugh.

The whole thing had been a very uncivilised affair and now it was getting silly and it had reached new depths,

I couldn't wait for it to be finally over and I could once again get my life into some kind of order;

But unbeknown to me at the time the divorce was to be the biggest life changing thing that had ever happened to me, it wasn't that it had changed my life so vastly,

Although I'm sure you can see it had, it was that I was, all be it unwelcome at the time being pushed into facing the daemons of my dyslexia, and this was to turn out to be a whole new beginning and it was to turn my life around for ever but not without a lot of heart ache and hard work.

Chapter 6

SO I'M DYSLEXIC!

It was a situation I knew I would have to face one day but I'd put it off time and time again it was too scary to own up to.
All I had achieved in my life to this point, all the house building, all the business achievements, all the determination, all the life changing things that I had been forced to face, and all the single mindedness of that faded into insignificance compared to this mountain that I was now to face.
But at least I could draw on the knowledge that I had gained from my past experiences to make this task a little easier.
After all, I had achieved the impossible, according to my critics.
And with that it had shown me that in fact nothing is impossible.

Most people can tell you what they think dyslexia is, they will say things like "its

people who have difficulty in learning how to read and writing" I wish that that was all there is to it, but there's so much more to it than that for the sufferer! At best people think it's just an excuse for being stupid and at worse they forget the excuse part,
I know;
I'm one of the unfortunate few!
Or could it be one of the fortunate few? I'll let you make your own mind up at the end of this book as you read on.
About the best I could do at this point in my life was just about write my name and address.
My hand writing was so bad it looked like a spider had fallen onto the ink pot then walked across the paper, it was all but illegible, and my reading was a real up hill struggle, the solicitors letters I was now receiving thick and fast would take hours for me to decipher,
That had to change and fast; I had been thrown in to a place I didn't want to be,

and I had been thrown in at the deep end head first; it was a dark and frightening situation to be in, so I'd got to teach myself how to read and write, but where to start and how? It was a part of my life that up until this point I had managed to avoid, but I no longer had a choice, it had to be faced and it had to be now,

I had to start somewhere so I started by spending night after night in secret trying to write what I'd done through the day, where I'd been, who I'd met, and what they had said then checking it with my word master,

In secret! as my shame was too great for me to let anyone know what I was up to, it was a start and stop affair,

if I had a visit from well meaning friends checking if I was OK coping with the stress and strain of divorce I would have to quickly gather my paper and pen and put it in the nearest drawer, put on the TV and make out I had been watching that!

I was so ashamed of my disability that most of my closest friends didn't even know, so I would only resume where I had left off when they had gone.

It was a long hard slog and nothing really made sense;
It soon became obvious that I was getting no where fast;
dyslexia is sometimes called word blindness and I was as blind as a bat;
The word master was a big help but I could confuse it with a regular monotony, if it could have talked to me I'm sure it would have said, hell I'm not a mind reader or psychic I'm a spell checker, and you must at least be in the right field for me to be able to give you any help!

A hand writing specialist would have said it looks like the writer had fallen into an ink well and had eight legs ,two of them at sometime in the past had been broken and now were deformed as a result, and it would have been easier if the writer had at least been sober! It's that bad.

The leap I'd taken was to big and to general, I was trying to run before I could walk, it was like you trying to learn a foreign language, its one thing learning how to speak it but a totally different ball game trying to write it and read it,

Well that's how it was for me but the language was my native English, and hell was I struggling!

If I could write it down then I couldn't read it, nor could anyone else for that matter, disheartening to say the least, but after all I was 36 years old and had never written a cheque in my life,

Paid a cheque into the bank,

Paid a bill, filled out a form, or written a letter.

A shameful admission, but never the less

the truth;
So this was it, my life changing shock and I was about to spend all the spare time I had for the next five years putting this right.

Chapter 7

School hadn't been kind or of much use to me; junior school hadn't been too bad! it was a small friendly place with approximately sixty kids in the whole school, I cant say I enjoyed it but I didn't mind it either, although I did get the feeling that I was somehow different from the rest of the kids by the way I would be left out of the lesson, but at that age its quite nice to sit and draw while the other kids in the class sit writing. Although it was a hell of a long time ago I can remember feeling alienated, but I could play as hard and as good as the best of them, I could run like the wind, kick a ball almost as far as Peter Edmons and he was the best ball kicker in the whole school, and I was dam good at colouring in! But that was about the extent of my education at junior school, and I really didn't care, I was having fun, that was all that mattered to me, and I thought that's what school was all about, just having fun with your mates.

But looking back I was obviously over looked, over looked is possibly the wrong way of putting it, more like misunderstood, I guess I was treated like I had a handicap, a kid with a handicap would be given something that they could do, and I guess that was me, but as far as I could see there was nothing wrong with me but I got segregated.

If the teachers did try to teach me how to read it wouldn't last long, they soon gave up and I was back happily drawing again, and they would be whispering to each other and glancing at me, I didn't understand but I did know it was something I had done but I didn't have a clue what it was, looking back I remember feeling uneasy in class the only way I can describe it is that I felt very alone, and as I say somehow different, it was as if the teachers could see something different in me to what I saw, but I had done nothing wrong! I would sit there confused and lost it was like I was a different person sat inside this body looking out that couldn't communicate with the outside world, I was intrigued as to what they were seeing but I was only a kid and your thoughts are not those of an adult, and the things I remember thinking were, I wonder if its because I'm fat? Are my clothes not as nice as the other kids? Do I smell? And I can remember thinking to myself that maybe if I had blond hair I would fit in a little better, the blond kids seemed to get all the attention so could that be it? My brother and sister are blond and they got a lot more time spent with them so it was blond I needed to be!

 The truth of that is they were easer to teach than me and whatever they were told they could take in but needless to say I didn't understand that, all I could see was that I looked the same as them but my hair was dark! Why me? Why was it me who had to be born with dark hair? I can only imagine what my parents thought when I told them I wanted to be blond and when they would catch me putting on my mum's perfume! As I say rational thoughts are out of the window when your six years old. And it didn't do much for my education.

At that time the eleven plus was still around but I had the day off as the rest of the kids did the exam, I couldn't even write my name so what was the point of taking any exam? But I don't remember any explanation as to why I wasn't doing the things the rest of the kids in my class were doing, but by this time I knew other kids could read and write and I would have day dream wishes that I was a normal kid and I could take the exam like the rest of then, but again I felt alienated and left out but at least I could ride my bike for the day and that was better than going to school anyway.

But then came secondary school, and it turned out that I would learn almost as much there as I had at junior school,
I guess moving up to secondary school is always traumatic for any kid;
Split up from your friends, new teachers, new surroundings, it was so big and unfriendly, with a smell of disinfectant, I had never seen so many kids in one place before, and with that fear of the unknown, all worrying stuff!
My birthday is September the first, the day I moved up to secondary school, I don't know how I had slipped through the net but the cut off date for the new term was and still is august the 31st, and by that reckoning I should still be in junior school,
But there I was it was my eleventh birthday, and I was the youngest in the year, a new school, so vast, kids everywhere all looking lost,

We'd all been herded in to the main hall about sixty or seventy of us, awaiting our fate like sheep at a cattle market, eventually the head master arrived, a big fat man with a booming voice introduced his self, my name is Mr Cromwell I'm the head master of this school, then started shouting out names of kids, and there allocated classes,

I watched as all my mates from junior school went to there classes;

my name eventually came up, over to b block room 6 class 4d, there I sat, room 6, b block, surrounded by what I can only describe as misfits and weirdoes, one kid sat there with florescent green snot running down his top lip straight in to his mouth without the slightest attempt to stop it, in fact I think he quite liked it by the way he would clear it away from time to time with his tongue;

Another sat desperately drawing pictures of bombs and giggling with glee as he quickly scribbled them out as they

exploded;
Another guy couldn't keep his eyes still; they would flick from side to side, so he would peer at you from the corner of his eye, the only way he could keep them still, and all the time he would be eating the top of his pencil with a nervous vigour;
A girl sat there deep in conversation with her imaginary friend, and judging by the smell of the room, more than one of them had personal hygiene problems;
With kids that desperately needed help, and they frightened me, I didn't know just what they were going to do next, or what they were capable of,
I didn't know how they would react to any given situation I had seen them explode, smashing chairs, throwing books for no reason that I could see and that scared me.

I guess I knew somewhere in the pit of my stomach that this was going to happen to me, but the reality was worse than any nightmare, although junior school hadn't been so bad but I had known since a very early age that there was something wrong or different about me, but this was a devastating shock, this wasn't how school should be! What had happened to the friendly atmosphere that I had been use to?

i remember thinking they've got me in the wrong class,

I'm not as bad as this lot, but most of them could actually read and write, but I still thought they would fetch me and put me in my real class, and every time the door would open unannounced in the middle of a so called lesson I would think this is it they've come to get me "I'm out of here," but they never came and with the misfits I stayed desperate and forgotten.

I started to dread school and all that it stud for, it became a situation that I hated so much, it was always on my

mind even while I was asleep, I would have night mares and that would only be after I had cried myself to sleep.
I just didn't understand why this was happening to me?
Why me?

And kids can be really cruel; I was never aloud to forget that I was in the misfit gang, the friends I'd had at junior school didn't want to hang out with a misfit, a retard as they put it, after all that would be real uncool;
So not only was I desperate and forgotten but alone now too;
One of the thing that school did teach me was to fight, I got sick of the name calling, so my breath taking speed and accuracy with which I could deliver a left hook became legendry, and I BECAME THE JOKER.

I found one of my skills was that I could always make people laugh. I would

always act the fool and that way people would like to have me around and I'd got some friends back!
 But that way I was living up to the perception people had of me, not only did people see me as a fool but now I was acting like one.

I couldn't read or write and without those basic skills I was stuffed, no history, geography, chemistry, not even metal work,
I did wood work because the bright kids got priority, ironic really as I'm a blacksmith and farrier now, I did go to the lessons initially but no matter what the subject there's always reading to be done if its either on the black board or from text books, and then writing from them in to your books, an impossible task for me, I couldn't even write my name so if it had been all written in Latin it would of made no difference to me, English or Latin it made no sense.

so I did what was called extra English, "extra English?" There was very little done in these lessons let alone English, there would be work set from time to time but it was a sham, a get out for the school. the class room was in an annex in the farthest corner of the school, it seemed that even the place was chosen so as to be as far away from the rest of the school as possible, tucked away in a corner, out of sight and out of mind, and again I sat there with the misfits while they dribbled drooled and stank, even the teacher wouldn't spend long in the room with us. he would only put his head around the door from time to time to see if we were all still there, but I cant say that I blamed him really after all the air was fresher out side, even though all he would do was stand leaning on the outside door chain smoking, probably the only time I wanted to spend time with a teacher.

But I was stuck in the class room with

the rest of the misfits.
It felt like I was cocooned in this shell trying to break free but always found myself back where I'd been put,
all of my childhood i felt lonely, and isolated,
I tried really hard to get out of that situation but if you can't read what's put in front of you, and cant write what you need to, what chance have you got?
It broke my heart but nothing changed hard as I tried;
I begged and pleaded with my teachers to get me out of there,
But no matter how hard I tried things just got worse, now I was a bigger problem to the teachers, I was kicking up a fuss and every one could see it,
I was making them look bad! Here was a kid that wanted to learn but they couldn't teach me, to this day I don't know if what I was asked to do was a punishment or a real effort to help, but when the other kids were asked to stand

in front of the class and read so was I! I was put up in front of these kids that I knew really needed help but who could read and write,

It felt that I was put there for there entertainment,

And how they laughed as I stood there with my book open staring at the page but it would of made as much sense to me had it been written in Latin. I couldn't read a dammed word of it so there I stood without saying a word as the laughter rang out!

That put a stop to my protesting, it was simple but very effective, a good session of public humiliation can put a stop to most things believe me! And I didn't really know just what an effect it had had on me until recently, when we where asked to do a small demonstration with the horses at a local show, great I thought that will be good and free advertising for our business, but then the bomb shell "I was to be on the microphone" the last time

I had been asked to speak in front of a crowd was back in school some thirty five years before and the fear was as real on this day as it had been back then except now I was a grown up with lots to say!

Came the day of the show and I was terrified but I knew this was something I just had to do for me!
"You know for my growth!"
Or maybe it was yet one more way to show the world that I was no longer that blithering fool that had been so badly humiliated in that class room so many years before!
Sid had come with us to lend a hand for the day and he must of seen my worry, are you worried about talking on the mic? He said,
Your dam right I'm worried, I don't know what I'm going to say or how I'm going to say it!
Looking me straight in the eye he said

hell fire if you cant blag your way through this then no one can, and you know he was right, I did it, it was informative and entertaining and at the end I got a round of applause, and now I sit here in front of my lap top searching for words to describe my complete satisfaction and joy at completing my first public speech "small as it was". but something's are just to big for words!!

I guess public speaking holds fears for most of us, we are all open to ridicule and criticism but my past experience had pushed me to take the microphone and do it!

As old and as wise as we get those experiences of our formative years are the ones that can freeze us to the spot but I'm one of the lucky few, I know that I'm damaged and as such I wont let that damage get in my way if that makes sense?

I had somehow always known that I could of gone one of two ways, I could of excepted what I had been told "good for nothing" and proved them all right and have achieved nothing and done nothing with my life or I could show all those doubters that they were wrong, I chose the latter but I have seen quite a few people who were told they, like me, were good for nothing and you know what? that's what they have done NOTHING although a lot of them have real talent in there hands but were influenced in there formative years that they were good for nothing and that is what they have believed all there life's, and they have let it hold them back, imprisoned in that downward spiral of doubt somehow set in stone when they were kids.

Me on the other hand, I went the other way, if anyone tells me I cant do a thing that just fires me up to do it anyway "whether I wanted to or not" and that's the way I've been since that day I gave up on school.

Chapter 8

My parents tried and were maddened when I became rebellious, skipping school, smoking and fighting, I'd managed to get away with the skipping school as that way I wasn't a head ache to anyone, and the teachers knew but they turned a blind eye, you know out of sight out of mind, but they demanded explanations when I almost got expelled for not doing my homework, and telling the teacher that if he would teach me how to read and write then I'd do his fucking homework, how much of this had I got to endure before someone would help me?

But it looked like I'd kicked a can of worms with my out burst of colourful language and got things moving at long last, and I guess things had got to come to a head sooner or later;
Soon after that a psychologist came to assess me, this was my chance, although I was scared and very nervous I really believed he would see what I felt in my

heart, after all he was a trained expert!
And he did, i did well in every test he gave me and at 14 my IQ was 127, "if that means anything at all" but it made things worse, I don't know if the psychologist had said it or the teachers had come to the conclusion themselves but now I was told that I was just plain lazy, and because of that I was an idiot for wasting my time and there's, "hell they must be right"!

All I ever got told was "your stupid, a fool, lazy, and backward" and that I would never be able to read or write; and of course my position wasn't helped by the fact that my older brother who as I saw it was a goody two shoes, who never got in to trouble, always did his homework, got on with the teachers and never answered back, and my younger sister, again a model student, who would get me into trouble for things I hadn't done just because she could, and in my words she was a creep.

I was endlessly compared to them, by my parents and teachers alike and needless to say neither of them suffered from dyslexia. "there was nothing wrong with them so I was just a bad kid with an attitude problem", it was at this point that I lost the will to fight, it had taken a long time for me to get the picture but I'd go it now;
" OK I'd got the picture!
Please please don't tell me anymore!
I hear what you are telling me;
please stop now!
I'm sorry!
I'm so sorry!

PLEASE PLEASE STOP, I CANT HURT ANY MORE THAN I DO ALREADY,

I know I am the cause of all this trouble;
I know that I'm responsible for the stress and heart break that I am somehow inflicting on my parents,

I know that I am the thorn in the side of all my teachers,
I hear what you say".
I was endlessly told by them in no uncertain terms that their life would be so much easier without me around, with comments like, things would be so much easier without you in my lessons, and this school would be a much nicer place if you were not in it.

It all amounted to making my life more difficult, both at home and school, hell how many times and for how long had I got to listen to this?
I had got to accept my lot,
the fact was that i could see i was guilty of all the things i had been accused of,

I could see that it was a fact that I was hard work for the teachers in the class room;
I was the rebellious kid, and the kid that developed an attitude; again all "fact"

I was the kid with all the lip and disrespect for all authority; again "fact"
I could see they were right; after all it was always my teachers that would ring home with complaints about my behaviour and never a word about my brother or sister;

I was all the things I had been accused of, so in my mind they must be right about me being backward, stupid, and lazy too. I had lost all my self worth, any belief that I had in myself was fast fading, the situation I was in was dire and it was all my fault, the guilt and frustration I felt was immeasurable but what could I do about it? Nothing! I had tried as hard as I possibly could but nothing had worked, I didn't understand why but I did know by now it was all my fault and i would carry a feeling of guilt with me to some degree for a very long time,
I guess right up until the time I faced my demons and then eventually when I

wrote this book;
Anyway that was it I gave up on school, what more could I do?
I'd hoped with everything I'd got that the tests would change things only to have my hopes dashed once again,
It wasn't that the education system didn't know about dyslexia it was that they chose not to acknowledge it.

I left school in 1975 a whole year before I should have done,
I was fifteen, but there was a twist, a sting in the tail and that was, now the education system threatened to fine my folks if I didn't go to school, crazy really as one of the parting shots from one of the teachers was that she would be pleased to see the back of me.

I had learnt nothing at school and I'd given up on it,
I guess a part of me started to believe that this was my lot as did every one around

me; it was assumed that just because I couldn't read and write that I was useless at everything.

The truth is I dug a hole for myself in search of affection, appreciation, love call it what you like, or just to fit in,

I knew I was a disappointment to every one around me, my dad just didn't understand my situation and couldn't really cope with the fact that I couldn't read and write (that sounds really bad but I cant think of a better way to describe it) after all my brother was his yard stick and there was nothing wrong with him, so he spent the vast majority of his time showing him the father and son things and I would hang around and catch whatever I could. Don't get me wrong he was never nasty or bad to me but it was that he was old fashioned and just didn't know how to handle me, he knew I was no fool but just didn't get it, he was very eloquent and had no problem with the written word; he just didn't understand that anyone could have problems with them, somehow it was beyond his thinking.

My mother had tried to help me, but she would almost always end up in tears, tears of frustration, and to see her crying because of me ripped my heart out, I didn't understand!
What could I do to make her as proud of me as she was of my brother and sister, so I'd do the menial tasks, like mow the lawn, wash the car, dig the garden, clear the lawn of dog muck, and yes it got me a form of appreciation, but the hole I'd dug gave the impression that was all I was good for, and as a consequence they were the jobs I would be given.

Chapter 9

The frustration i felt inside would somtimes burst out and I would end up having a paddy shouting and cry
as I look back that could have been when I lost the spirit to shine and come good, had it not been for that voice in my heart that had been with me for as long as I could remember, telling me they'd got it wrong, and I was so much more than mowing grass and shovelling shit,
years later I read a saying that goes,

IF YOU ALWAYS DO WHAT YOU'VE ALWAYS DONE YOU'LL ALWAYS GET WHAT YOU'VE ALWAYS GOT,

and for years I did what I'd always done and always got what I'd always got, so I was in a hole and without being able to read and write that's where I stayed until I was 36 years old and my divorce shot me in to unknown territory. Don't get me wrong I'd proved my worth in many things, as I've already said I'd built my house brick by brick, I'd plumbed it, wired it, and plastered it, the lot, a little ironic really as one of Jane's main gripes was that I never stopped working and it was as if I had got to kill myself with work before the world would see that I was not good for nothing, and I have to admit she was right I didn't; and I had got to prove to the world I wasn't good for nothing, still to this day I don't really know if that is what cost me my marriage, but I'm sure it went a long way towards its demise;

I had my own business that was doing fine, I had managed to get an apprenticeship as a farrier, about the only thing I could do without any qualifications, it was hands on and very hard work and I got good at it and I could make good money from it, but I had never faced my reading and writing daemons,

If I was going to show my worth it had to be now,

The alternative was to fall back in to that hole even further, and the thought of that was to scary for words.

So this was it and failure not an option, The memories of school and my childhood gave me all the motivation I could ever need to teach myself how to read and write. I can still see the faces of the teachers as they told me i was good for nothing and would come to nothing, the look of disappointment on my mothers face, the gut wrenching feelings as I'd over hear conversations between my parents, and between my parents and teachers, that would go like "I don't understand, his brother isn't stupid" or "there's not much point going to parents evening there not going to tell us anything we don't already know",

as I write about those days, it still hurts almost enough to stop me writing

but if I do that kid who was me might not be understood, that unintentional abuse will carry on, and hell I know how

that feels, and for all those people who doubted me, and for that kid with the bright eyes and big personality, who doesn't read or write so well,
For all those teachers who think they have all the answers,
I hope they read this book and have a greater understanding of that intelligent kid with dyslexia and know a little more about how they really feel.
In my view I was robbed of the most basic education, the education that surely every kid is entitled to, but I was robbed just because I didn't fit in, I was there nightmare, a kid that was different, I didn't fit in to there education strategy, I was the difficult kid, I was hard work for them and they didn't like that, I was left in no illusion as to how they felt about me, as one teacher told me I was a boil on the backside of his class.

As hard as it remains for me to say out loud or even write, in my adult life I by no means consider myself stupid or limited.

I have a vast interest and understanding of numerous things ranging from architecture, mechanical engineering, structural engineering, aviation history, nature, art, and the list goes on, but as a result of my lack of education, I became a farrier. A good enough job and I've managed to build myself quite an enviable reputation at being very good at my profession, and its served me well. At one stage I was given the opportunity to teach my trade to college students, but you guessed it I had to turn it down because of my dyslexia, but had I an education things might have been different, I could of saved my body from the physical strain of 30 years shoeing horses, I could of used my brain a little more and a little less brawn. Or even the choice would have been nice!
But I had very little choice, think of it

what job would you give a man who cant read or write?

I think its quite clear that he's not going to be a news reader, an editor of a news paper, a teacher, or a post man, he wouldn't get a job as a van, bus or lorry driver, not if you wanted him to go any where in particular and find his way back, how could he if the road signs were to him all gobbledygook? You couldn't even trust a man like that to stack shelves at the super market, not if you wanted things in there right place that is. Just think of all the things we do in the course of our lives that involve reading and writing and we take them for granted! Reading baked beans on a tin is almost a reflex to most of us, but to a dyslexic it could be a ten minute job, and for that dyslexic who really needs a job its just one more brick wall that's impossible to clime.

People tell me what a wonderfully romantic job I have, and ask if it's a family profession, was your dad a farrier? He wasn't, he was an engineer; and then the question so why a farrier? My answer is always the same, freedom to be my own boss, to be out in the fresh air, and I meet very interesting people, and I guess that's true in part, but the part I omit to answer is that I have made the best of a bad job as regards my education and I really had very little option.

After all these people respect me for what they see so why tell them the truth and spoil that.

And as for the Romance! Its bloody hard work,

But I guess people see the post card image, the sunshine, the great out doors, and the nostalgia;

And yes there are not many days that I don't appreciate the freedom of being my own boss,

The job satisfaction,
And the sometimes breathtaking scenery in the Peak District on the edges of the Pennines; with the morning mist rolling along the valleys on early summer mornings, and the beautifully lazy and historic market towns, sleepy villages with there old world charm and rustic architecture;

The crisp frosty mornings of mid winter, with the magnificent variety of wild life in north Derbyshire which makes me realise things could of turned out a damn site worse for an illiterate like me;

But then again there are days when I wake to hear the wind hammering the rain against my window, and I know I'm going to get soaked to the skin, covered in mud, and if I'm really unlucky my work for that day will be a string of shire horses on beely moor, and that's no easy task I can tell you, when the average shire horse ways about three quarters of a ton and I had got to support a quarter of that weight at any given time while putting his shoes on, and I had to do this while the rain comes down horizontal, and the lazy wind up there blows right through you, lazy wind as it's known because it's to lazy to go around, and that's in June! It gets really nasty in winter, at that time of year the wind will cut you in half never mind blow through you! And with a frost so sharp you could shave with it!

And then the late summers days as the day's work is coming to an end the sun low in the sky,
There under the spreading chestnut tree I shoe the last horse of the day; the rhythmic chink of the hammer on anvil;
The sizzle of the hot shoe as it's fitted to the hoof;
The smoke gently drifting up through the branches;
The healthy tanned skin and arms of iron, sounds romantic hey?

But the bit that's not on the post card is the midges, that never give up on me, or the horse, my blood shot eyes, after repeated thrashings from the horse's tail as it tries to keep the insects at bay, and from the sweat constantly running in to them created by the heat off the hot shoes, the blistering temperatures of the mid summer sun, and the shear physical exertion of the work; "only fools and horses hey!"

And yes arms with muscles any body builder would be proud of, but I can tell you the bigger the muscles the greater the aching pains;

Hardly being able to stand upright after being bent double under horses for eight hours a day, with aches and pains of almost thirty years shoeing horses!

With injuries sustained in that time ranging from nails ripped through my hands;

Knocked out by highly strung over fed pampered ponies;

Torn ligaments, broken bones, kicks, bites, shat on, jumped on, and almost castrated, knocked cold by ponies with no manners.
I CANT SEE MUCH ROMANCE IN THAT!

As you can see there are good sides to my work and bad, but my career options were greatly reduced by my non existent education, and In my job I've met a lot of very interesting people, ranging from professors of engineering, through solicitors, doctors, business men, builders, and farmers, and most have become good friends, and all are educated people and that's when I can see just what I missed out on with my education, but having said that I know that my past is what's made me who I am today. i now believe that if another man can do it then so can i,
and I will tackle anything, after all I was told I would never be able to read or

write, good for nothing and come to nothing and more than likely end up in prison, I guess there's time yet for the prison I'm only forty-nine, but can I just say that I have no police record if you don't take into account speeding tickets, not that crime wasn't an option I know it was, and it was a close call. I could of ended up in a life of crime, I guess I could of rebelled big time and got into all sorts of trouble, after all that was what the world expected of me, but there was one thing that saved me, and that was that voice, that feeling in my heart that had told me for years and years that they had got me wrong. As I've said, if your told something over and over for long enough you get to believe it, and I had been told for so long that I had no hope of ever achieving anything worthwhile that I almost believed it, I was all but convinced, had it not been for the unrelenting feeling in my heart, I was going to say it could have been down to the toss of a coin as to which way I turned but in truth I couldn't or my heart wouldn't let me go down the road of crime.

i had got to show them all that they were wrong,
and again the truth is I really wanted to make them eat humble pie.
So I worked hard saved even harder to afford a range rover, this was all happening in the late seventies and range rovers hadn't been around very long at that time they were a status symbol and I was obsessed I had got to have one, and after four years saving I got my pride and joy, a beautiful gleaming white range rover. As I look back I can see it was a trophy a way for me to say to all my doubters "UP YOURS LOOK AT ME NOW" I was young and bitter, but it felt really good. I wanted to drive it up the school steps and park it on the grass at the front of

the main building, but I never did I guess I got a grip of myself just in time, but I had achieved something not only had I got my flash car but obviously a good job which enabled me to afford it, and it gave me a buzz just to prove them wrong.

but then I couldn't stop, I set myself bigger goals now I needed a house, not just a house but a house that would say wow look at him now,
I found and bought a cottage in a well to do village that needed extensively renovating, I was already working like a dog putting in 12 and 14 hour, seven day a week to show the world I was not good for nothing and to be able to save for the deposit on my house. I was 22, the people I had been at school with were working 8 hour days and still living with mummy, but here I was I had got my flash car and a van for my business and now I had a cottage of my own, but

in reality the cottage was a shell and I would have to rebuild everything on the inside. It was a long hard job but I was obsessed I had to get it done and stuff the world, and I did but there was a blissful moment, as I was in the midst of all the renovation, it happened one evening in summer I was walking my faithful mutt Mac, a black Labrador, through the village when I recognised a face in one of my neighbours gardens. It was miss Johnson the teacher that had told me she would be pleased to see the back of me and the very same person who had said I was good for nothing would come to nothing and would probably end up in prison, I couldn't help myself, I made a point of talking to her and said that I didn't know she lived in this shit hole as I did, I know it was childish and bad of me but it was to good a chance to miss, and man it felt so good! But my determination to show the world that they had made a bad assessment of me got to be an obsession, "not that I could see that was what I was doing at the time" but I had tasted success and I couldn't stop, I did my cottage up and sold it to finance my next project, I wanted to build my own house, and that was when I bought the 15 acres of land over looking the derwent valley, and again the truth is that project was yet another trophy to enable me to stick two fingers up at the doubters and say take a look at me now, take a long hard look now who's good for nothing?

Then came my divorce which changed my perspective on life, the one thing that I had been fighting against had once again surfaced and jumped up and bitten me but this time I had to face it, as I've already said I was left in a desperate situation regarding my literacy, but my marriage had failed! And I had to look at all I had done, all I had achieved, all the work I had put in over the years, I guess its all a part and parcel of divorce but I had to ask myself what was it all about? Had it all been worth it? And for a while I blamed every one else but slowly it dawned on me that it was the chip on my shoulder that had ripped my life apart, but once again it wasn't just that simple, yes I had that chip on my shoulder the one that had pushed me to the point of destruction to prove to the whole world that I was no fool, I had sacrificed many things in my quest for recognition, like holidays, hobbies, leisure time, family time, even my son had to work along side me to get my affection.

It was a hell of a shock, but I don't take all the blame for the brake down of the marriage, its only when I look back that I can see it would of failed no matter what, I can now see we were two different individuals with widely different interests, I did and still enjoy the same things I always did, nature, I can watch a buzzard slowly sercoling over the hills and fields of Derbyshire for hours, I still look in wonderment at the magnificent architecture and engineering of some of the buildings and bridges that were built over 200 years ago, the engineering that made great Briton great, but now I take life at a much slower pace, to allow myself to indulge in the things I enjoy.

On the other hand I hear of the life Jane has picked for herself, all the things that would drive me insane, night clubs till 4am, karaoke, parties, crowded places, holidays, two weeks in greece lying on a beach all day, and all night in a night club, all the things that would bore me to tears. As I say two different people heading in different directions, so I guess the marriage was doomed from the start, but now I had to look at what I was doing and why, questions I asked myself like, how long did I have to prove my worth, and did it prove my worth to all that had doubted me and were they really interested anyway? it had become a way of life for me, but the divorce had taught me an important lesson, no matter how hard or how long you had worked for your goals they could all be taken away a dam site faster than they were gained.

Life goes on and it was high time I started to live mine for me, and the determination I had to show the world I was no fool I would now channel in to the things I enjoyed, after all what more had I got to prove? the things that were just for me and not to prove a point any longer, the difference is now I make the time and use that determination to change the way I do things, after all it had served me well while I had used it to show everyone else they were wrong about me so now I would use that same determination that had pushed me to build the house to teach myself how to read and write,

And with that same determination to write this book,
That's me; I was told for so long that I couldn't do this and that, so tell me now I can't do a thing, I'll do it just to prove you wrong, even if I have to break a gut to do it.
And for so long I was in that cocoon, relying on myself, and had to fend for myself, that now I find it hard to allow anyone in to my world, what can they do for me that I can't do for myself?
rightly or wrongly i believe we all ultimately stand alone,
and if we want things to change in our lives then its down to our self to change it, anything is possible if we want it bad enough and try hard enough;
But what I had undertaken was possibly the hardest thing I had ever had to face.

Chapter 10

After I had left school I sort specialist help, but these so called specialists spend more time arguing between them selves as to who's got the right theories, and trying to disprove all other theories that are not there own, and while they argue the dyslexic "me" sits in the middle learning nothing, well that's the way it looks to me anyway!

And at the risk of sounding bitter, it appeared to me that every so called specialist I have ever listened to will spend as much time, if not more time telling me about other peoples theories and how they were all wrong, and why they were wrong, and less time convincing me his way was the right way, it leaves me wondering if somehow the in fighting could be stopped would the ultimate goal be better achieved?

after all we as dyslexics or parents of dyslexics are interested in results,

We don't give a dam who thinks they have the right theories, we need proof, and we need results "plain and simple"
We don't need to hear the infighting just show us results that's it!

my specialist help had failed,
and It was just one more nail in the coffin of the psychological destruction that was my dyslexia; it had just confirmed to me that I was beyond salvation, and it would be another twenty years before I would be forced to face it again.

But the fanciful theories carried on without me, and all this achieves is to give parents a modicum of hope that at least something is being done for there kids,

but when it becomes obvious that it's not the miracle cure they had expected the despair comes back bigger and stronger than ever, which makes the task for the dyslexic kids even greater, now he or she knows they have a big problem, they must have as now they are getting specialist help! But the worse part is its not working, so now they know they must have a real problem!

Put yourself in the position of that kid, he's a happy go lucky chap, and quite smart with it, he can talk walk run and play as well as the best of them, "probably better" and he doesn't have a care in the world as far as he knows everything is fine, then the bomb shell is dropped,
first he's told he has a problem, which is a shock, but then he's told not to worry because we will get this expert in and everything will be fine!!!
but after months of one to one tuition the situation isn't "fine" at all, so now that kid that was happy playing with his friends, and who was care free has now been shown that he has a big problem, and the psychological rot has started, and the unintentional abuse has begun.

you don't have to tell a child that his mum and dad are disapointed.

no matter how they try to cover it up the kid will always know, imagine how that kid would feel if the situation got to a point where mum and dad started falling out about how the situation was progressing or not.

As adults we understand it's only natural for any mum and dad to be concerned about there kids education and we put our faith in these so called experts, but I left school being able to write my name and that was about it! I did enrol for private one to one tuition after I left school but even that made no difference so I quit.
I'd got through thus far relying on firstly my mum and then after I got married on my wife Jane, but now I was alone 36 years old and not about to go running back to mummy!

it seemed to me that everywhere I turned and everything I tried to do, there was some kind of form for me to fill out.

I was now faced with all the things I'd managed to avoid for so long, but I had no option I couldn't ignore them any longer,

Even the things that should have been simple were made complicated and scary by my lack of experience, the things that most of the world consider easy and never think twice about were very challenging to me, like booking my work in to my diary, where I was going and what I was doing.

And then writing the receipts for the work I had done;

Taxing my van!

I had to find the registration and insurance documents then there was a form to fill out, that is if I could read it in the first place, and of course a cheque to write;

Christmas and birthday cards with funny verses; as I'm seen as the joker my cards were always humorous and it was something I would dread, I'd kept my secret from most people but this was one of the situations that could of quite easley court me out and exposed my inadequacies, as I was handed the card I would be expected to read it, I would quickly try to get a clue from the pictures and gage what my reaction should be by them, should I laugh out loud or was it a sarcastic card and should my reaction be a sneered smile?
and it didnt stop there,
other day to day things like-
Reading road signs, an impossible task at any greater speed than walking pace, you try slowing to that pace when your half way around a roundabout or on a motor way!
That in itself could turn out to be a life changing situation if you try it!
And then the forms, so many bloody

forms to fill out,
Going to the dentist, a form!
The doctors, a form!
The bank, a form!
The solicitors, a form!
The accountant, a form!
The post office yet more forms!
Opening an account at the local garage, a form,
The dam things were everywhere,
Even my son's school had forms for me to fill out,
And every one of them was a public place where I could be exposed to ridicule and humiliation.
You can imagine the embarrassment when someone asks you how to spell a word that is a part of your address and you just don't know.

Reading birthday and Christmas cards was almost impossible but writing them was impossible!
Finding my way around the Derbyshire

countryside was a major task in its own right as I couldn't read what the road signs were trying to tell me, navigating by the stars in the middle of the day can get difficult believe me;
even today I have to remind myself to read the signs, I know that must sound strange but it's a habit that I just haven't got the hang of yet.

Mobile phones had just become the new way of communication, a fine piece of kit but with them came text messaging, just one more thing to challenge me!
And I would live in fear of the postman dropping mail through my door, it would be another bill that I couldn't pay if not yet more letters from Jane's solicitors,
The daemons were around every corner just waiting to catch me out and show the world just what a fool I really was, **and the first time i'd used my debit card!**

simple hey?

Well may be for you!!!

But I'd paid cash for everything I'd ever bought so as to avoid the embarrassment of saying to the shop keeper I couldn't write cheques or fill out a form,
As I say I was now living alone and I'd ran out of food, washing powder and toilet roll, I was due a visit from Sid but I had nothing in the house to feed him with; I'd paid whatever bills I could with the cash I'd got, and things were getting desperate, the freezer was empty, the cloths basket full of dirty washing and the wardrobe empty of clean ones;
I guess I'm stubborn but I wouldn't be beaten,

But I did weaken and ask a very good mate who I knew wouldn't laugh at me, how I used my debit card,
Then off to the local supermarket, what

could be simpler than handing over the card and signing the slip (one of the things I could do) then off with the groceries!

That's if of course the shop had the same symbol on the door as I had on my card then I knew I was OK, I could shop there, and again of cause if I had enough money in the bank to cover it, but I didn't have a clue if there was ten pounds in there or a thousand, so I had to take the chance, I had to blindly trust that it be OK,

Picture this; I'm 6 feet tall, 15 stone, and at the time I had a beard that was dappled with grey to match my hair and it all had got a little out of hand,

I'd been busy shoeing horses that day and it's not the cleanest job in the world, with work boots covered in dried mud and jeans to match, not the best a tier for shopping, I hadn't even changed my old thread bare wax jacket that not only stank like a horse but was covered in horse hair too;

Looking back I must of looked like some kind of tramp, but that was the last thing on my mind, I was worried daft about using my debit card, silly I know but it was totally alien to me at the time,

After two or three laps of the supermarket trying to ignore the strange looks I was getting from judgemental housewives and staff alike,

I'd got washing powder, shower gel, bacon, bread, toilet roll, fish fingers, coca cola, and biscuits for Sid, it's a good job that most of the packaging on the groceries had pictures of what was inside other wise I could have ended up with anything! You know if it had got pictures of beans on the tin then chances are that's what's in it, but not always! I had got what I thought was lemonade but in fact it was tonic water!

But anyway now to pay for it, so to the

check out till;
The place was packed but eventually I got to the front of the queue, I put my goodies on the little conveyer belt and then packing them in to bags, the cashier said something like that will be £34 please, I handed over my card with confidence, only to be met by what was to me a mind bending question,

"do you want any cash back,"

Pardon? I said; my heart skipped a beat as the thought ran through my mind, "shit there's no bloody money in the bank and she has sussed me! How the hell am I going to get out of this one?"

"do you want any cash back?" said the cashier once again

You've just said that, what do you mean I thought I paid you?
I hadn't been warned that there might be

an alien on the cheque out, apparently what she was asking me was common place but to me she could have been talking Swahili,

What she was asking me just didn't make sense,

Here I was trying to pay for my groceries and the cashier was trying to give me money?

i really didn't have a clue what she was talking about,

Surely if there was no money in the bank she would of said that!

Well she said if you need some cash you can get it here rather than making an extra trip to the bank,

Oh I understand now,

What a relief! Was that all now my heart could resume its rightful place back in my chest;

No!

No thanks, I said.

By which time half the shoppers had

stopped what they were doing and were watching my antics, they must of thought I was some hill Billy or a grizzly Adams look alike, who had just nicked the card,
how were they to know i was as innocent as a child on the inside.

I'd managed to embarrass myself and make a real prat of myself too, but I had got away with it and I'd learned a very important lesson, I wouldn't be caught out again, not by that one anyway.
But this heart stopping experience had shown me that this just couldn't carry on.
As I walked from the shop my heart was pounding and I was shaking; shaking so much that when I had got back to my car I could hardly get the key in the lock, When I had eventually got in I sat there for a while in the sanctuary and security of my car I was safe, what a relief,
but as I sat I thought to myself hell I'm a

big strong man now but I had just frightened myself half to death just by doing my grocery shopping,
what kind of state was this to get in!

I felt like that kid again
I had just reopened the emotional wounds of my childhood,
It hurt and it was scary.
But I had got away with it! still no one had any idea of my plight, I had managed the walk out of the shop with my pride.

As I'm sure you can see and understand there's a stigma attached to not being able to read and write, and I'd spent so long bluffing my way through sticky situations I wasn't about to tell the world now, my pride just wouldn't let me and I had grown sick of the whole situation, that fear of someone finding out about the real me, the ducking and diving when I was faced with situations that could expose me was getting me down, it was becoming hard work,

So I had no option but to somehow resume my quest to teach myself how to read and write, "but how" and where do I start?

My main worry was how would I pay the bills? I'd got the money in cheque form but firstly couldn't put them in the bank, and then if I had I couldn't write the cheque, or fill out a bill! And the last thing I could do with was the bailiffs coming to take the few things I had left.

And if that wasn't bad enough my tax returns were looming ever closer, hell how could it be that I could find myself in such a state?

I'm sure you can see I was in a desperate situation,

DESPERATE SITUATIONS CALL FOR DESPERATE MEASURES.

Chapter 11

Over the years I'd learned how to read a bit so I wasn't totally lost. But now with dogged determination I set about my task, and as I've said what a task, I really didn't know if I would be successful, everything else I had achieved had been tangible things, and this was completely different.

What I needed to do now was learn how to write and spell, and I needed to do it fast! But I'd already tried and confused myself, I had to try again but this time from a different starting point, My first priority was to be able to write a cheque, so the start had to be numbers, armed with my word master (a pocket sized spell checker that would spell the word and tell you what it meant) and a calendar, one, two, three, four, five, checking every word as I went, I was doing fine until number eight! Eat? Ate? Eait?

i'd managed to confuse the word master and i was stuffed!

It was around 4am when I eventually found it on of all things my marriage certificate! We had got married in March 84, EIGHT? That doesn't even look like eight never mind sound like it! And what's all that ght business about? But at least I could get some sleep now! I'd spent almost 6 hours learning how to spell up to eight!?

I'd started and the next day my work got in the way, people would say I looked tired and that I would have to stay away from the ladies and get some sleep ALONE! and I'd say things like yes I know she's killing me or that's the price you pay for being single and free, and I got quite a reputation for being a ladies man, but it meant I didn't have to make up stories why I looked so tired, they were doing that for me.

I had honed my skill at being witty; I've always got a funny answer, some kind of wise crack that would put people off the scent, and I must admit I had got really good at it, so much so that I wasn't always sure what was the truth myself, but I knew I had got to keep my secret to myself for now at least. I knew that if I was to face ridicule now it would of made my task even greater, so my secret was kept with me, if only they new the truth, but I wasn't about to tell them now, and I guess if I had told them the truth they wouldn't of believed me anyway, I had blaged joked laughed and fooled my way through so many sticky situations they would of thought I was fooling around anyway, but the fooling around had to stop when I returned home, but through the days work I couldn't stop thinking and worrying about spelling and my predicament, That night the same again, starting at one again, over and over for the next few months my life existed solely of shoeing horses and writing, checking it as I went,

PROGRESS WAS SLOW AND SOMETIMES MIND BLOWING WITH FRUSTRATION.

The only person that I would permit to see what I was up to was my son Sid, although I didn't tell him what I was doing he somehow knew! And one night when his mum had dropped him off he ran upstairs gathered his early learning books together and spread then across the table in front of me! And said I've been thinking dad, and I think these will help you!

It was a fantastic thing that he had done but he was only seven years old and shouldn't be worrying about me,

I just didn't know how to react, on one hand I was touched by his thoughts and the offer of his help, but on the other I was gutted that at his age he was worried about me! as I have already said you don't have to tell a kid that there is something wrong, he had seen me struggling and wanted to help, and the truth is his books did help, but only by the fact that I could see that they were intended for people without dyslexia. It was all good stuff but a for apple, b for ball, c for cat, d for dog and so on is not much help if you cant tell the difference between a "b" or a "d", sure it told me how to spell those words but without the book in front of me I was stuffed, It didn't help me recognise the letters, a "b" could still be a "d", so as I say fine for a kid without dyslexia but not much good to me.

So back to it one, two, three, four, five, over and over, slowly progressing to teens and so on, but as I saw it eighteen should be spelt eightteen, but I had to accept it was one of those strange things about the English language that didn't make sense and it was that strangeness that helped me to remember if that makes sense, and I had to carry on regardless, the more I did the better I got until I had got to one thousand, big deal I hear you say but to me it was like winning the lottery. I can still remember the first cheque I wrote, it was for diesel £35, or I should say thirty-five pounds only. I can still remember that feeling, can you imagine asking the most beautiful girl out in the whole school, you'd wanted to ask her for months then when you plucked up enough courage she had said yes!!

Enough to make you do somersaults around the playground, I wanted to do somersaults across the garage for court, I didn't! But I did feel 'eight' feet tall, it felt that good!

Now I was getting somewhere, I'd got a result at long last!

It had taken me months to get this far, to this point my quest was like a drug and now I was addicted! I needed to learn more and more! I needed answers to problems that had plagued me for years,

like why was it so hard for me to write a word and remember it?
And was I doing something wrong?
or more importantly could i do something different that would make it easier?

Other people had learned this at junior school and here I was at my age slogging my guts out to make headway and I was, but if I did something different would it be easier?

Chapter 12

WAS THERE A KEY TO DYSLEXIA?

And if there was would I ever really crack it?

I was making head way so I must be doing something right as I thought, but my next move left me gutted and disappointed, I'd gone back to what I'd done through the day and writing it down, but I was as abysmal as before! I'd attempt a word get it wrong spend all that evening finding the right way but by the following evening I'd lost it again, and no matter how many times I'd written it the previous night when I came back to it I was never sure,
what had gone wrong?

What was I doing, or not, that I had done with the numbers? Back to the numbers, and to my amazement I could still do them! This wasn't making sense at all, why could I remember how to spell numbers? After all they are just words to.

Nothing was consistent or predictable. some nights I would get a word right first time I tried, but the following night get it wrong, but I always had to check it with the word master, what the hell was going on?

Strangely it wasn't all words that I had trouble remembering, things like cat, dog, wall, tree, I could remember how to spell and read, but somehow I got stuck on innocuous little words like, and, if, it, of, as, so, in, why should this be? And if you add to that 'I'm told' the problem with dyslexia is that the brain doesn't process letters correctly so a '**b**' can be a **d, p, q, g**, or **9**, and an '**s**' a **5, 2**, or even a '**z**', an '**e**' can be a '**3**' and a '**w**' could be an '**m**', a '**j**' can be an '**L**' or even an '**f**'.

so not only were the letters back to front

but upside down to, or even both back to front and upside down! It was a mine field of confusion but I could see some truth in this as I was never sure if a **b** was a **b** and not a **d** and so on.

I'll try to explain!

Imagine if you could pick the letter **b** off the page and throw it across the room as it tumbled and spun it would be all the letters I quoted **b, d, p, 9,** and **q**!

if you were to throw an **S** it would be as it spun a **2** and an **S**.

W would be an **m** and a **w**, before it landed,

I realised I couldn't distinguish between any of them on the page, not really.

as I said nothing made sense, but it wouldn't would it!

And it is hardly surprising that the word master would get confused, if I had put a word into it that started with a **b** but I had put a **d** without recognising it the machine wouldn't be able to help would it?

you can only imagine my frustration at this, but without recognition of the letters this was what I would do time and time and time again, and the dam thing would return words that were nothing like mine, and I would question weather the thing had broken.
Some nights would be a complete waste of time, I would achieve nothing! In fact I would take two steps backwards, and three back, I would reach a point of despair, on more than one occasion, in fact more times than I care to remember! I just had to trust and hope I could make up the difference the following evening.

It was only when I got given an old computer that I could see my mistakes, if

I had spelt a word wrong or used the wrong letters it would underline it in red, but now I could try to correct it as it sat on the page in front of me, and after a while it became obvious to me that I was spinning letters around;

I don't know if it was that you can grow out of dyslexia, my desperate predicament or my inquisitive mind, and I don't know how I had stuck it for so long, but now I could see myself using **b's** as **d's**, **p's** as **9's**, WHY? Or not so much why as how can I stop myself?

I had discovered what I was doing and I was pleased to find out, but how the hell was I going to correct it.

If I could somehow find a way to recognise a letter surely this would help me make sense of it all?

it became obvious to me that just writing a word over and over again wasnt really

the answer.

yes it had worked for me to a point, now I could spell numbers as well as a 9 year old could be expected to, but clearly that was just the start, and was a lot of what I had done just down to luck? Luck that I had managed to get the letters the right way around; after all I had with most of them a 50% chance of getting them right anyway!
And was I really getting the letters the right way around? After all I was away from my word master and the people who read my writing might just be being polite and not telling me!
So from the elation of that first cheque, "quite an achievement in its own right" to the stark reality that I still had a hell of a long way to go;
So now I knew what I was doing! But how the hell do I make a b, a b, and not a d?

And if I did it with **b's** and **d's** what other letters do I do it with? If I could crack this then surely life had to be easier!

So where from here? Back to the start AGAIN, a b c d e f g h over and over and yes I got better but I was never 100% sure I was right, there had to be a way I could be sure, but how?

I made a list of all the letters I thought could be reversed inverted spun or twisted.

a b c d e f g h j k m n p q r s t u w y z.

Then a list of letters that could become different letters if they were twisted around.

A **b** can be **d**, a **g q** and **p,** and they could all become each other.

An **f** could be **j** if its turned on its head as **j** could be an **f.**

A **g** could be a **6** and its already a **9**.

M can be W, W to an m.

An **n** can become **u**, and vice versa.

An **s** can be a **2** and of course a **z**.

A **t** can be turned and become a **y**, in some writing anyway.

It seemed to be so elementary to me that first of all the letters should be made distinguishable from each other before I could move on.

In fact it seemed so elementary that I thought I must be wrong!

Surely if I was right it would be where you would start with a kid that had dyslexia, but I couldn't remember anything like it when I was a kid,

and I've since learned that its not really addressed properly today.

But this was my struggle at the time and I had to find answers to it,

so I worked out a plan that if I wrote a

simple word that had in the case of **b** and **d** both those letters in it, it had to be a word that I knew how to spell, not too big or complicated, then I could see a **b**, and a **d** side by side then remember the word! "**bed**" was the word, if I had the head and feet in bed I knew I'd spelt it correctly and I could see the difference between **b** and **d** at a glance.

But if either the head or feet or both were out of bed I knew I'd got it wrong, simple but very effective.

Now I knew the difference at a glance and with time and a lot of practice I found myself writing **b's** and **d's** without really thinking.

I look at this as anchoring the letters down, to stop them from spinning unrecognisably, and it works with every letter.

It's just finding the right word with the relevant letter!

as I said **b** can be **d** and an **s** can be a **2**, **p** can be **9**, a **t** can be a **y** and so on, so now to find a word that is; one, easy to spell, and two, that you can make up a story about, a story that you can easily remember.
But that was not as simple as it sounds!

I don't think it's a new thing that I had discovered,
In fact I do know that the word bed has been used before, and I don't think it's a new technique, but it did become obvious to me that the word that was used was critical, I could see that if the word was set by a non dyslexic to be used as an anchor, it could be more of a hindrance than of any help, what makes sense to a non dyslexic makes no sense to a dyslexic, and vice versa, so the big advantage I had was that no one had told

me how things should be done and I could make my own way, slow and hard as it was.

Another big advantage I had was that I now new what I was doing with the letters, although it was extremely frustrating it was a big key to solving my dilemma.

As I say an **S** can be a **2** to a dyslexic it can also be a **Z**, as in the letter **b** or **d** the story to that is if you can spell bed but just don't know a **b** from a **d** deb to a dyslexic does say bed, as bed can say deb, if you imagine that one little word in a sentence,
"I'm going to deb "it not only doesn't make sense to the listener it makes no sense to the reader.

I'll try to write a sentence as a dyslexic might see it,

"yh3 bog ran yo hi2 deb anb lat bomn",

What it should sound like is -
"The dog ran to his bed and lay down",

heavy going, huh?

"Good" now you have a little insight into what the dyslexic would be seeing, and that's just one manifestations of how it might look there could be hundreds, try again and see how you do,

Wuw wad3 dreakfasy yhi2 worning for u2 anb m3 had jaw on yoasy,

Or the same sentence in a different manifestation to give you a better chance of getting it right,

Muw mag3 qreakjasy yhi2 worninb jor u2 and w3 ha9 faw ou yoazt.

Do you want me to tell you what it says?

Have you tried?
Have you really tried?
Its easy go back and try again,
Ok I'll stop playing teacher now, it says,

**mum made breakfast this morning and we had jam on toast.
So did you get it?**

Or are you really stupid?

Sorry I was just trying to make a point, it's not easy and you're not stupid it's very confusing, and it was never going to make sense to you, but it really is a good representative of how that sentence would have looked to me at least.

As you can see I've changed the letters, **m** in to **w** **b's** in to **d's** **p's** or **9's** **t's** in to **y's** **j's** in to **f's** and **s's** in to **2's** or **Z**, as I say that is just two examples manifestation of how it could be, **b's** and **d's** could be **9's g's** or **q's, s's** in to **z's** or **5's** and so on, or even any permutation of any of them, and they could be all different in the same sentence, I guess there must be some mathematical equation that could tell us just how many different permutations there could be but we can imagine without that that its going to be a hell of a lot, it could be that nothing is the same twice, but one thing is for sure its a mine field of confusion and frustration!

So when I could see that this was how I would or could be seeing things it became obvious to me that this had to be where I concentrated most of my efforts and without question it's where I needed to start, how could I progress any further with a handicap like that? And at this point I would like you to think just how difficult it was for you to read that simple sentence and you had been warned that it was going to be gobbledygook,

BUT NOW IMAGINE THE AMOUNT OF EFFORT THAT A DYSLEXIC WOULD HAVE PUT IN ONLY TO GET IT WRONG

and for that person not to recognise any difference, and imagine a kid sat with his/her teacher trying to read and make sense of that with the blind leading the blind! "Impossible"
And to think I'd been labelled as stupid and backward because of that!!!!

To make things worse I realised to that I could see the subject, but not always the word, out of that first sentence there was only one word I would of made sense of "bog" I could see wet mud, you know a bog, a swamp, but it had not the slightest relevance to what the sentence was trying to tell me, and what was worse it hadn't even said bog at all, no wonder my reading was naff I was reading things that werent even there!

There had to be a link, was that why I found it easier to spell numbers but not all day to day words, I could see a number it had a picture, but words like "where", "what", "when", and "how", do not, could that be what is meant by word blindness? It was as if I needed to be able to see the subject before I could relate it to the letters on the page, so back to it, could I remember how to spell words with pictures?

And the answer was yes, the easy ones anyway, dyslexics see in pictures not words, to picture a bed with the **b** as the head board and the **d** as the foot board with your head and feet in bed makes more sense than mere letters on a page to me, and what's more it looks like the real thing, a lucky choice on my behalf, but other letters wouldn't be so easy.

So on to other letters such as **S**, again 2nake can say snake,
If you think about it and try to pronounce 2nake it would sound like twnake, clearly not a word, no wonder nothing was making sense!

Six is a good word to use as an anchor if the **X** is a kiss and the **S** is a snake blowing the kiss over the I the **S** is always facing the right way, which not only tells me what's an **S** but also alternatively a **2**,

M's and **W's!** that was a hard one for me to solve; mow is the word I used to anchor then down, **Mow** is 2 and 3, the **M** has 2 peaks and **W** has 3, I can see **Mow** and spell it and I can count, as simple as that,

As I said I could now see myself using b's as d's, s's as 2's or 2's as s's, and m's as w's but imagine a child of six or so with dyslexia wouldn't see it or even know the difference! She/he would see just what she/he saw, as I had done for all this time.
how could any one be expected to write or spell with that handicap?
Some letters are more difficult than others, or should I say more confusing than others, the letters that gave me more stress were the letters like b and d, the ones that can be when reverted inverted or twisted different letters, t to y's, m to w's, s's to z's, p to q's, and so on. And obviously an o is always an o, an I is always an I, an L is always an L, and an x is always the same no matter which

way around.
And there are the ones that cant be made into anything else, an **a** is always an **a** no matter which way around, as is **c**, but never the less very confusing.

Chapter 13

I had reached a turning point in my quest, I now knew what I had been doing for all this time and I had worked out a way I could anchor letters down.

I remember my own school days teachers would get me to write b a hundred times then turn the page over and I'd more than likely write a d the same letter to me, and once again I was told, "and you guessed it" I was stupid, lazy, backward, and good for nothing, "again" as if I hadn't heard it enough.

This began to infuriate me beyond belief, you would only have to insinuate that I was not quite as bright as you and I could flip into a rage, I guess its like your dog if every time you walk past him you keep poking at him with a stick eventually even the nicest natured dog is going to bite you, and to my mind you would of asked for it, but the next time that old granny walked past with a stick it would bite her to, but would that then be the dogs fault?

I since learn that Albert Einstein, Richard Branson, Jackie Stewart, even royalty, and many more well known and famous people are or were dyslexic and no one could accuse them of being stupid.

So I made the decision that i would never again call myself stupid,

not even in fun, every one else had done that for long enough and although it had gone in to what was by now my make up I still didn't believe It anyway, **SO I STOPPED!**

And strangely this helped with how I felt about myself, I didn't understand why at the time but I have since read (because I can now) an article about the way our minds might work, and it said that we have a conscious mind and a subconscious mind, the conscious mind is the one we reason with the one that can work things out, and the one that can distinguish between the truth and a lie, and the subconscious mind is the one that that locks the door behind us when the conscious mind is busy working out the best way to get to work or the shortest route to the shops, it's the one that checks that the traffic light is on green when our conscious mind is thinking of the things we need to get from the shops, as it says it does the subconscious things, its like our built in computer, it cant reason it only knows and believes what we tell it weather that is right or wrong, so if we tell ourselves that we are stupid it believes us, and then as a consequence restricts us from reaching our full potential. So after stopping calling myself stupid I started to believe that anything was possible, I started to believe that I wasn't in fact stupid, sounds daft I know but it really did help.

And after all it was time that I started to take care of myself, I'd had enough of the hard and heartless name calling from everyone else, so it was time that I looked after myself, it was high time I protected myself from the name calling rather than adding to it.

Call it what you like but I believe that if you tell yourself for long enough that you are incapable of doing a task then you are beaten before you start and you will in fact fail.

I guess it all comes down to being positive or negative, and positive is always best.

As I continued with my quest of getting to the bottom of my reading and writing problems it became more obvious to me the teachers I'd had just didn't see the problem, how could they after all they weren't dyslexic, they were as confused as me, the saying is you have to live it to know it, and I'd only just found out myself what I was seeing so how could I expect them to help!

As a kid your teachers are a kind of god no matter what they are telling you, and when those gods are calling you stupid, disruptive, and backward, you get to believe them, although deep in my heart I knew they were wrong, so there I was I'd found a key to a part of my puzzle that worked for me but would it work for others?

Chapter 14

A friend of mines 14 year old son "john" was dyslexic and having specialist help so I tried it on him;

I got him to write the word **best**, the only word I could think of that had most of the letters that I knew he could get wrong, and after a lot of persuasion, he wrote **de2y** and looked at me waiting for an answer to see if he had got it right, what could I say?

If you take on board what I say about **b** being **d** and **s** a **2** he had got it right, he could tell me how to spell it, **b e s t**, but wrote it like that! (So much for his specialist help!)

"I told him he had got it right but just used the wrong letters"

I showed him the bed and snake story, and had to think fast for a word that would make a **'t'** a **'t'** and not a **y**, as I say thinking fast, tit was the word,

"How many girls had he seen with them sticking out the back?

I got him to write the anchor words then after turning the page, asked him to write **best** again, right first time and every other time after too, before he'd looked to me to tell him if he was right, but now he knew for himself, without me saying a word.

He was so proud of himself, his confidence grew there and then, his stress had gone with just getting one little word right.

He wanted to do more and more, at last he had got someone who could understand and show him how.

To be truthful I'd learned as much from him as he had from me, but the part that shocked me the most was that john was still suffering by the same misunderstanding that I had experienced some 25 years earlier,

I thought dyslexia was better understood now days, but by this example, that was clearly not the case and after all john was having so called expert help! So I asked what he would do with his special teacher. I couldn't believe that what I was doing was so revolutionary but it had worked with john so what had this teacher been doing? And it wasn't a surprise to me to learn that the teacher had missed the mark, although what he was showing him was to a point relevant, john told me that most of his time was spent trying to learn what sounds letters made when alone and when they were put with other letters, like an o on its own made a different sound to two o's when they are put side by side, and he would be given repetitive training, he would get him to write a letter a hundred times in the hope that it would somehow teach him which letter was what, but that's all it was hope, there was nothing technical or useful in what he was doing that I could see anyway, and nothing had changed. He was doing the same things with John that my teachers had done with me when I was at school and i knew for a fact that it didn't work,

and he was missing the point just as my teachers had, of course its relevant to know what sound letters make but if you don't recognise the letters in the first place it's a futile exercise trying to put sounds to them, and it can only make matters worse, he was obviously over looking the problem, or he just didn't know that a d to a dyslexic can be a b, and if you just don't recognise the difference, the sound they may or may not make is surely irrelevant! Until such times as he knew the difference it would be a waist of time trying to show him; I could see it was the blind leading the blind and nothing was ever going to make sense for john until such times as he could recognise the letters put in front of him, how would he start to read if the word said book and he was reading dook? "isn't a dook a bird that lives on the water?"

The first job is to anchor the letters down and then learn what sound they make, johns teacher had missed the start and without that he was just making things worse, the more john tried the more frustrated both he and his teacher became, neither of then knew where the other was coming from, and what they were doing was making it harder for both of them, and with it more and more stressful. I was struggling to see what specialist help this guy was giving john, one of his words of wisdom to john was if a letter looks right it is right, and if it flows then it must be right,

"AND THIS GUY WAS BEING PAID FOR THIS?"
in my opinion he wasn't doing his job in fact in my view he was doing john more

harm than good but it wasn't up to me to tell him, and who was I anyway? I had no formal qualifications and more than that I couldn't read or write that well myself so at that I had to leave it and concentrate on my own reading and writing before I could help anyone.
But a few weeks later I bumped in to johns mum and asked how he was getting on with his dyslexic classes, I guess I was after feed back from her as to what I had told him? But she was very dismissive of what I had shown him, saying that what I had shown john was nice of me but his teacher was a trained expert and that she was putting her faith in him, so more or less I was told that my help was not needed! But you know the sad part is that john left school without even taking any exams and is now a farm labour! Not that there's anything wrong with being a farm labour if that's your choice! And I know it wasn't johns, he wanted to be a heavy goods vehicle

fitter, but that is now a distant dream.

I don't blame johns mum for making the decision she did, if indeed she had a choice, she knew as much about dyslexia as she did about rocket science, and after all she had fought long and hard with the school, and the education authorities to get some help for john, and now she had it, she wasn't about to give that up, no one could blame her for putting her trust in the British education system, and holding on to that trust with both hands.
I'm not saying at the time I could have made a better job of things for john but hey I don't think I could of done much worse either!!

I had learned a lot from john, it had shown me that the so called experts that had been sent to sort me out were as useless as John's so called specialist today, and I could see that John knew in his heart that the help he was getting wasn't working, and I could see it wouldn't be long before John gave up altogether, but It had showed me that pressure and stress were a really big key to blocking a kids learning ability. I could see John's pressure and stress had stopped him writing for me, and it was only when I told him that he had no need to be ashamed or worry as I wasn't a teacher but I was the same as him, I had dyslexia to, and whatever he could do would be really good because he was helping me.

And when I told him he had got best right the first time he wrote it, but just used the wrong letters, his attitude changed now he was a little more relaxed and willing, it wasn't that I'd intentionally lied to him it was that I believed he had got it right but used the wrong letters, I guess if I had put a big red cross next to his work then the lesson would of been over no matter what I had said.

It had shown me that I could see de2y said best but it was that he didn't recognise the letters, and that had been me, even though I hadn't realised it at the time a t could be a y, and it taught me that I was on the right lines.

Now I needed more anchor words for every letter in the alphabet,

I guess I cheated with the letter **p**, again a **p** can be a **9** but I could see a nine so a **p** had to be the opposite, and the more nines I could see together the better, so I use **1999**, to remember a **9** and alternatively a **p**, or **"apple"** again I can see an apple, is green and red, it has a picture and I can spell it,

so when I look I can see an **a** and a **p** side by side, which gives me both an **a** and a **p**, to me they stand back to

back, "apple".
Tit with them proudly facing forward not only gave me a t but again alternatively a y, another word to anchor t's and y's is toy, again its easy to spell it has a picture and it gives two letters in one word, and the story: If the o is a ball and the y a netball basket and the t is you throwing the ball into the net the y will always face the right way as will the t,
I mentioned earlier that dyslexics see in pictures!
I didn't really understand why it was that it was easier for me to spell or remember how to spell words with pictures, I thought everyone saw things in pictures as I did.
how do I explain, now I've got the hang of reading and writing I recognise words

where as before they were just a collection of letters, and the letters weren't even the right way around, non dyslexics see the word, recognise it and say it, we see pictures not a collection of letters, or at least we need a picture for us to relate the letters to, I'll explain,

not all words have pictures.

Take dog - that word has a picture; others like "tree", "ball", "cat", "wall", "door", "bell", tangible things have pictures,
If you think of a dog you can see a picture of it, a collie poodle or even a great Dane, whatever the dog it has a picture, but other words have no picture like "the", "it", "at", "is", "yes", "no", "but", "of", "are", "know", "where", "was", "this", "that", all have no pictures,
as much as you try you will never picture an "of", its all very confusing to a dyslexic, especially as the dyslexic doesn't know that's what they see, its

like your personal computer, you ask it to search for an item press search then wait; in a dyslexic the computer comes back with "nothing found" for words without pictures, but while the dyslexics computer has been busy looking for a picture that doesn't exist the gist of the sentence is lost,
Other words have pictures but the wrong pictures or at best misleading pictures,
Like "and", the computer returns "hand" or a "knot" in a rope for "not",
All managing to confuse the reader,
Other words have to be accompanied by yet more words before they make a picture, like over, jumped, and ran,
Jump has to be accompanied by a skipping rope or kangaroo, and ran could have a tap, or someone running for a bus,
Now the computer is heading for melt down, and the words it once recognised are gobbledegook to,
If I put them in to a sentence and then

explain,

The dog jumped over the wall and ran across the field to get his ball; the words with pictures are, dog wall field and ball,

Words without pictures are, the, to, get, and,

Words that need to be accompanied to get a vague picture are, jumped, over, ran, and, across, and his,

Now if I only use the words with pictures it reads like this,

?Dog ? ? ? wall ? ? ? ? field ? ? ? ball,

If I write it using accompanied words but using misleading pictures along with the picture words, it reads,

? dog jumped over ? wall hand ? a cross ? field ? ? ? ball,

You can see it doesn't make much sense, imagine how it would be if you had to first picture the words, then accompany other words with yet more words before you got there pictures,

That small sentence becomes a confusing mountain to climb, then imagine being eight years old with your teacher breathing down your neck!

All pressure and that only makes things worse.
I'd spent a long time trying to sort this problem, again one way was to write lists, after all it helped with the letters, so obviously checking as I went, and I started with the easy ones, well the easy ones to me! The ones I had less to worry about, The words with pictures; dog, cat, field, ball, tree, house, wall, and so on, then to words without pictures, at, as, of, off, if, it, is, where, when, what, was. Then on to words with misleading pictures, and, hand, knot, not, sore, there, their, then I studied them long and hard, adding to them as I studied, but all I found out was there's a hell of a lot of words that don't have pictures, and just as many that have misleading pictures.
I must of spent months on words without pictures, trying to give them

symbols for me to remember them by, but that only made things worse, I could remember the symbols but then couldn't remember the words I had put them with. I tried all sorts of things but nothing worked, and words with misleading pictures, again the same, but I'd spent little time on pictured words as I thought at the time they were my friends and the least of my worries, but in reality it was the pictured words that were creating the problem, as I say after studying the other two for months I turned to the pictures words, and they were still easier, but it struck me could it be that I looked for pictures for every word subconsciously, and was I just confusing myself? So as an exercise I tried consciously not to look for any pictures no matter what the word as I read, and it was better, so now I had to look at the picture words, and after being my friends when anchoring letters down, now they had become my stumbling blocks, it wasn't that I had to forget them but just remember not all words had pictures, and not to waist time and effort looking for then, and just with that my reading got immeasurably easier,

things were starting to fall into place for me now!

i now realised that not everyone saw things as i did, "in pictures"

I had always thought that I had developed the skill of watching things done and rerunning them in my mind when I needed them, like a blind person would develop there hearing, there touch, and like a deaf person would develop there sight, but maybe not! Maybe it was that I see in pictures anyway, and it was a skill I was born with, "a gift" after all a picture paints a thousand words, so maybe a non dyslexic would have to read a thousand words to get the same picture I would get, and they would have to store them! But all I had to do was store a picture, so a thousand pictures = a

million words, not only can I look at an individual picture in my mind but I can run the film and watch it as many times as I like until I understand, I can watch the film hundreds of times so when I come to do the given thing its like I've done it a hundred times.
Was my life easier than there's?
If you take on board what I say it had to be, in all but the written word, but after I put together every thing that I had learned it was only now that I realised I could really learn how to read and write, the same as a non dyslexic.

But the English language is one of the hardest and most complicated to learn, and it was to be a monumental task at my time of life,
Now I had reprogrammed my computer; I'd learned that for all this time I hadn't realised that letters had been spinning uncontrollably, or that I saw words with pictures, I hadn't realised that I would

ask my computer for pictures for every word weather they had them or not, I taught it how to anchor the letters down, I only ask it to give me pictures to words that have pictures, or more importantly I don't bother it with trying to find pictures for words that don't have them, and I had to learn all those strange things like where to use **ght**, where to put silent **k's, b's**, and **w's**, when a **y** became an **ie**, when to put an **e** on the end of words and when not to, I had to learn things like what sound **ch, sh** made; when to use **ou**, and not **oo**; and so on, all the things that most of us learn at junior school I had got to painstakingly learn from scratch, but at least now I could learn the same as a non dyslexic would of done, and I learned that dyslexia isn't about spelling at all. Although I wasn't good at spelling, that was the same as anyone, and I couldn't blame dyslexia.

Chapter 15

Whilst in the midst of all of this, I learned that one of my long standing customer's daughter was dyslexic, and its a story that I have been told many times of a really bright kid with a big personality, "Zara" she could hold a conversation with anyone; she would put forward very valid points, and always ask questions, I only found out that she was dyslexic by being in the right place at the right time, I'd gone to shoe a pony for Julie Newman, I'd shod for Julie for some 25 years and I first met Zara as a baby, Julies bump had gone and a pram appeared with Zara in it outside the stables, but now she was 12 years old,

Hell doesn't time fly!

Julie was not her usual happy self and being of the nosy kind I asked her what was wrong? Only to be met by a flood of tears, its zar zara sh shes dys dyslexic, I must admit I wasn't ready for that, well not the tears anyway, after gathering myself I said but Julie its not the end of the world! I know but I don't know what to do or how to help, I've had the school on the phone this morning and they say that Zara's dyslexic, what am I going to do?

Well Julie I might be able to help you there;

With that the tears stopped,
"how? how can you help?"

Well I'm dyslexic and I've been trying to sort it for the past few years and I think I might have cracked it!

You? Dyslexic?

Yes me dyslexic!

I told her all the things I had been up to, how I'd anchored letters down to stop them from spinning unrecognisably, I told her about **b's** and **d's, p's** and **9s**, all the things that I'd been working on, and I said I would have a word with zara if she wanted,

My revelations were met with disbelief it wasn't that she doubted what I'd done or what I was telling her, but that I was dyslexic in the first place;

Saying things like but your ok, and there's nothing wrong with you,

The reaction I would of expected but my concerns were with Zara and I wondered if I could help,

"I don't know but I would be really pleased if you would try; anything would help", so the meeting was arranged for one evening that same week,

I knew Zara wasn't worried about me, we'd had many conversations about lots of things but that evening she was stressed and worried,

So I told her as I had with John that she had nothing to worry about as I was

dyslexic which made me as good or as bad as her, she showed me some of her writing and I could see that she was having problems with **b's** and **d's** **w's** and **m's** and **s's** and **2's,** so I showed her the anchor words, got her to write them, and it worked she got them right every time, I told her about words with pictures, words without pictures, and words with misleading pictures, she understood immediately and volunteered words that had pictures, words that hadn't, and words that had misleading pictures;
She had got it and I was her new best friend

I've had subsequent conversations with Julie about zara, and its obvious to me that Julie is a very caring mother but one little talk I had with her revealed a detrimental side that she would have on zaras ability to learn, as I say Julie was very caring and determined to help her daughter however she could; in one conversation with Julie she had told me that she would sit with zara most nights and help her with her spelling, so what do you do to help? I asked even though I don't really think that spelling is anything to do with dyslexia, I think when the letters have been anchored down and after the pictures have been dispelled the dyslexic can learn just the same as anyone else, but I asked the question anyway, well she said,

We sit with maybe eight or ten words and I read them to zara and she will write them on the page, then I check them as she writs them,

I knew how keen Julie was to help but there was a part that concerned me, although on the face of it sitting and reading words to zara whilst she wrote then down was all good practise, but I also knew just what presser and stress can do to a dyslexic when they try to spell or read, it makes the letters spin even more vigorously and you revert back to looking for the pictures again, its like a reflex, so I asked Julie what she would do if zara got one right?

She looked at me with a puzzled look on her face as if to say what difference dose that make or even the answer was obvious, she said I hug her and kiss her and tell her how well she has done, "why" she asked,

ignoring her question I asked so what do you do if she gets one wrong? Again she looked at me with that puzzled look the answer was clear to Julie, I tell her how it's spelt she writes it correctly then we leave it, and say we'll try that one again the following night, " why"

So I asked no kisses or hugs then?

No said Julie with that look once again,

 As I say I'd already realised that stress was a big hurdle for the dyslexic to over come along with all the rest, and what Julie was doing to zara was adding to her stress levels, so hard as it was for me to tell Julie I said the contrast between right and wrong spellings are to wide, and once again I got the puzzled look as she said what, I don't understand?

I pointed out that Zara was putting as much effort into every word and she wanted her mum to be pleased and hug and kiss her with every word but she knew she must firstly get then right, but when she failed at best she got nothing and at worse that disappointing look from her mum when she had tried so hard to get it right, so the affect on zara was a slap in the face, no hug or kiss this time, and that equals disappointment and rejection, so the next word is so much harder so much more stress involved in getting it right which in itself reduces the chance of success, and then she's in a spiral of confusion and anxiety, I pointed this out to Julie and she could see what I was saying and said hell i've been

slapping her in the face every time she gets one wrong,
well yes I said but its easily remedied, how's that? She asked, I told her to be less extreme between right and wrong, and remember zara is trying just as hard for every word weather or not she gets them right,

We still have conversations about dyslexia, and she will ring me from time to time if she is stuck with an anchor word, she tells me what she is doing at school and how its helping or if its not, one of her concerns recently was that she had to read out loud in one of her special reading lessons, apparently the class consists of about eight or ten students and they have to sit around in a circle and take it in turns to read there section of a book, and if she got stuck on a word the other students would snigger at her; As she was telling me my blood started to boil with anger, hell I said that's public humiliation! Yes I know I hate is she said, without going to the school and strangling the so called specialist teacher, there was only one way I could help her, I told her that the next time she was up for public humiliation she had to tell herself not to look for pictures for the words weather they had them or not, and make a conscious effort to just read the letters on the page, after all she had learned how to recognise the letters and get them the right way around, and that she was not to confuse herself or waist time looking for things that are just not there.

The next time I went shoeing for Julie I was met by zara running towards me shouting, it works lance it works,

what works zara what works? It had been some time since our conversation and I had forgotten but it soon came flooding back when she said "the public humiliation and not looking for pictures, it worked it worked, thanks Lance thanks",

"hold on a while" I said "it was you who did the reading not me"!

"Yes I know but what you said really helped, thanks", she was so pleased and proud of herself, she had grown in confidence, I was so pleased for her it put a lump in my throat, but it occurred to me that there was a bad side to this; and that was that now her specialist teacher thought that what she was doing with her public humiliation was actually working, although this no longer effected zara in the same way as it had, but what concerned me now was that was no help to the rest of the kids in the public humiliation circle, but there was nothing I could do about that apart from hope that zara would talk to the other kids in the class and tell them what she had learned, but I could see there wasn't much likely hood of that now she had an advantage over the rest of the sniggering students and I could see she wouldn't give that up easily.

I think one of the best things I could of heard was that she had just started equestrian college and taken a draft copy of this book with her to inspire her, **to hear that pleases me beyond belief,**

and reminds me how far I've come and how it was before,

When I attempted to read a sentence I would start well but as I got further in I would slow almost to a stop, and I would have to read it over and over to understand what it was telling me, but now I read at the same pace and understand what I read the first time, nine times out of ten anyway.

Chapter 16

There is always a price to pay and mine was my family, you would think they would be pleased for me, if not proud, but the truth is they couldn't accept I had changed, I guess they didn't understand, and I know they couldn't see that they had always treated me like I was the family fool, and I guess there's always sibling rivalry in any family, firstly as kids, who can run fastest, jump the highest, and so on, then as adults, although we try not to but its always in the back of your mind who is doing better than who;
who has the best job, the best house?
The best set of important friends and the like.

I had shown myself that I wasn't a fool, and wasn't going the be treated like one any longer, and that saying passed through my mind once again, if you always do what you've always done you'll always get what you've always

got, they were doing what they had always done, but were getting a different reaction from me,
After all it was me who had worked hard and alone, in secret to change my life, and they were treating me as they always had and it was only me who could see what they were doing, and IT WAS ME WHO HAD SAID "NO MORE", and it was me who had changed,
don't get me wrong I wasn't nasty but I did stand up for myself, in my view if I had an opinion it was just as worthy of airing as there's, but this was alien to them and it didn't go down well, I'd always been spoken down to by them, but now I had an opinion!

"who did I think I was?"

They couldn't accept me as an equal I'd always been the fool and that was the way they liked it, and it was to late for them to change,

They would say with a sneer you've changed, you're not as nice as you were, but all I was doing was acting like an equal and they didn't like it,
I tried to explain, I told them how hard I had worked night after night to change my life and why, but I guess old habits die hard and my explanations fell on deaf ears.
Whilst trying to explain I made the mistake of saying I was going to write this book to help others with dyslexia, only to be met with howls of sarcastic laughter,
You! Write a book? Don't be stupid you've only just learned how to read yourself hee" hee"
I hadn't changed that much and all I would of liked was to be treated as an equal but it was never going to happen.
now I had a decision to make, was I to swallow my pride and be that fool they all knew and loved, or did I say no more, and the decision had to be that if they

couldnt accept me as i am then i had to walk away,
if they couldn't be pleased for me, then I had to turn my back, hell that was a hard and heart breaking decision, and one I wish with all my heart I didn't have to make; but I walked away, no big bust ups it was that I didn't go running when they said, I had my own life to lead and it was just as important as there's, and I'd learned to say no, where as before had they asked I would of jumped, I'd always been mr muscles for them if they had had a big dirty job to be done then it was me they would turn to but now I would say no I'm sorry I'm to busy, as I say no big bust up, what I felt like saying was I've been your labour for to long and now you can do your own dirty work, but I didn't I just didn't jump when they expected me to.
In truth the only difference to me was that I don't see them on a day to day basis, I still see them from time to time

but now it's usually at my mothers when our visits coincide, and even then it's a situation of one in and one out, unfortunately these times are now years apart.

I'd always stood alone, relied on myself and that hadn't changed,
But I had come a hell of a long way, to far to fall back in to that hole, that hole that now was closing up by the day,
I'd been to hell and back learning how to read and write, and I'd cracked it so I wasn't about to give up on that now, but it had taken me on one hell of a roller coaster of a ride of emotions,
And as I'd travelled on my journey I'd learned so much more than just how to read and write, id learned so much about Myself!

i'd asked questions i'd never dared ask before,
and I found myself digging deeper into

my past than I had really been prepared for and I'd come out the other side stronger and more confident, I now held the key to my destiny and I wasn't about to throw that away.

I'm now free, free from oppression and control, it's hard for me to explain! But as I see it people are taught boundaries, where things are black or white, the right way or the wrong way, and nothing in-between, the way they have always been, but the truth is things change, life changes, and its not always for the worse, my life has change immeasurably; and I'm immensely proud of all those things that would of frozen me to the spot with fear in the past that I now do without much of a second thought, I can now write a cheque, fill out a form anywhere, go to the bank, and I now question what I'm told and what we are taught,

I didn't have the brain washing at school, if that's the right way of putting it, if this doesn't sound too silly but if I'd not had dyslexia I wouldn't of been able to teach myself how to read and write, a daft thing to say I know but I had no one telling me to do it this way or that, no one to confuse me with there so called right way, I had no egotistical teachers ramming techniques down my throat, I was free to make and solve my own mistakes,

As I talk to people about dyslexia and teaching pupils with it, it becomes more and more obvious to me that even the most modern and up to date teachers have very little understanding of dyslexia, examples I experienced lately were when I told a current teacher I'd taught myself how to read and write, and her reply was

"you taught yourself?

you can't do that!

you've got to of had a teacher"

And the other also a teacher and the head of the dyslexic department, of an all boys school told me that his boys only spoke when spoken to, and that he demanded respect from them or there'd be trouble! The best tip that he could give me and the tip that he was giving to his dyslexic students was that if your writing didn't flow then you knew it was wrong, and he offered no more useful information than that, how dose he keep his job?

The first teacher was very limited with her assessment, or very arrogant to think there's only one way to learn anything "her way" the way it says in the book, if that's the case then **why is it we still have kids leaving school without being able to read or write?**
And the second who rules with a rod of iron and his way is the only way, surely respect is earned and not demanded?
And as for his useful tips that turn out to be completely useless to some one who

knows how dyslexia really feels.

All I can say is I'm glad I'm not one of the boys in his school not aloud to think for themselves,

It sounds more like we should be sending in the S.A.S to save them all, before they all turn into mindless robots unable to think for themselves, and the worst part is I'm talking of teachers in the twenty first century. What happens if a bright kid just doesn't get it, are they banished to the dunce's corner just because there teacher is limited to just that one way of teaching? or is it any wonder that teenagers after the oppression of a school that treats the kids like robots come out and take to drugs or run wild when they are given there freedom?

The experience I've had recently is that when I tell teachers how I solved my puzzle they are all very interested but the vast majority just cant see past what they have been doing for all of there careers, but if I tell a dyslexic they get it almost instantly,

I know I'm generalising and I know that there are a lot of very Good teachers out there who try very hard in difficult situations and bad circumstances, and I know there has to be a format to work to, that has to generalise;

but in the world of the dyslexic nothing is black or white,

and to make matters worse I don't think two dyslexics are alike.

For years and years I wanted with all my heart to fit in, to be in the so called box,

in fact I would of sold my soul to the devil to be with every one else, but now I consider that I had a close shave, hell I could be in there with all the limitations that brings along with it!

I question everything, no one is better than me or worse for that matter, but I know it might sound condescending but I do feel sorry for some people, unable to see that they are walled in by what society has inflicted on them.

Chapter 17

BELIEVE ME THAT DYSLEXIC KID MAY NOT KNOW WHAT IS GOING OFF BUT HE OR SHE KNOWS ITS HIM CREATING PROBLEMS, AND WHAT WAS A HAPPY GO LUCKY KID BECOMES SAD AND CONFUSED,

SO FOR THAT KID WHO JUST DOESN'T UNDERSTAND WHAT IS WRONG,

FOR THAT KID WHO IS AS BRIGHT AS A BUTTON BUT JUST CAN'T READ OR WRITE SO WELL!

WITH THE HOPE THAT THAT KID WILL BE BETTER UNDERSTOOD AND WON'T BE FORCED TO FACE HIS SITUATION ALONE.

TO TRY AND GIVE A LITTLE INSIGHT TO HIS TEACHERS AND FAMILY JUST HOW HE MIGHT BE SEEING THINGS!

AND TO SHOW THEM HOW THE WORLD LOOKS FROM HIS PERSPECTIVE!

TO TRY AND HELP REDUCE HIS HEART ACHE AND PAIN!

TO TRY AND SHOW THAT KID HES NOT ALONE!

<u>FOR THAT KID WHO WAS ME I WROTE THIS BOOK.</u>